Arduino best 10 measurement, Calculation and monitoring projects with easy approach !!!

Arduino best 10 measurement projects with easy approach !!!

CONTENTS

CONTENTS

ACKNOWLEDGMENTS

The writer might want to recognize the diligent work of the article group in assembling this book. He might likewise want to recognize the diligent work of the Raspberry Pi Foundation and the Arduino bunch for assembling items and networks that help to make the Internet of Things increasingly open to the overall population. Yahoo for the democratization of innovation!

INTRODUCTION

The Internet of Things (IOT) is a perplexing idea comprised of numerous PCs and numerous correspondence ways. Some IOT gadgets are associated with the Internet and some are most certainly not. Some IOT gadgets structure swarms that convey among themselves. Some are intended for a solitary reason, while some are increasingly universally useful PCs. This book is intended to demonstrate to you the IOT from the back to front. By structure IOT gadgets, the per user will comprehend the essential ideas and will almost certainly develop utilizing the rudiments to make his or her very own IOT applications. These included ventures will tell the per user the best way to assemble their very own IOT ventures and to develop the models appeared. The significance of Computer Security in IOT gadgets is additionally talked about and different systems for protecting the IOT from unapproved clients or programmers. The most significant takeaway from this book is in structure the tasks yourself.

1.BATTERY VOLTAGE INDICATOR USING ARDUINO AND LED BAR GRAPH

Batteries accompany a specific voltage limit and if the voltage goes past as far as possible while charging or releasing, the life of the battery get influenced or decreased. At whatever point we utilize a battery fueled undertaking, at times we have to check the battery voltage level, regardless of whether it is should have been charged or supplanted. This circuit will assist you with monitoring the voltage of your battery. This Arduino battery voltage pointer demonstrates the status of the battery by sparkling LEDs on a 10 Segment LED Bar Graph as per the battery voltage. It additionally demonstrates your battery voltage on the LCD associated with the Arduino.

Material Required

- Resistor (100ohm-10;330ohm)

- 10 Segment LED Bar Graph

- Arduino UNO

- Potentiometer-10k

- LCD (16*2)

- Battery (to be tried)

- 12v connector for Arduino

- Associating wires

Circuit Diagram

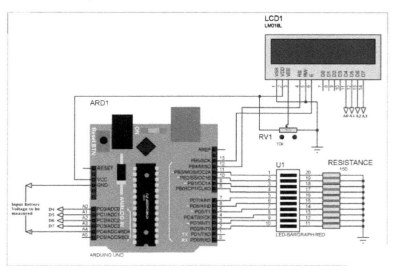

LED Bar Graph

The LED reference chart comes in mechanical standard size with a low power utilization. The bar is arranged for radiant force. The item itself stays inside RoHS consistent rendition. It has a forward voltage of up to 2.6v. The power scattering per portion is 65mW. The working temperature of the LED reference chart is - 40? to 80?. There are numerous application for the LED reference diagram like Audio hardware, Instrument boards, and Digital readout show.

Pin Diagram

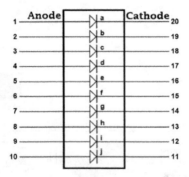

Pin Configuration

Pin	Function	Pin	Function
1	Anode a	11	Cathode j
2	Anode b	12	Cathode i
3	Anode c	13	Cathode h
4	Anode d	14	Cathode g
5	Anode e	15	Cathode f
6	Anode f	16	Cathode e
7	Anode g	17	Cathode d
8	Anode h	18	Cathode c
9	Anode i	19	Cathode b
10	Anode j	20	Cathode a

Arduino Program for Battery Voltage Monitoring:

Here, we are characterizing the LCD library and determining pins of LCD to be utilized with the Arduino. The simple info is taken from stick A4 for checking the battery voltage. We have set the incentive as Float to get the voltage up to two decimal.

```
#include <LiquidCrystal.h>

const int rs = 12, en = 13, d4 = A0, d5 = A1, d6 = A2,
d7 = A3;

LiquidCrystal lcd(rs, en, d0, d1, d2, d3);

const int analogPin = A4;
```

```
float analogValue;

float input_voltage;
```

The cluster is made for doling out the pins to the LED visual chart.

```
int ledPins[] = {

2, 3, 4, 5, 6, 7, 8, 9, 10, 11

};      // an array of pin numbers to which LEDs are attached

int pinCount = 10;      // the number of pins (i.e. the length of the array)
```

Setting up LCD and the simple pins (A0, A1, A2, A3) as OUTPUT pins.

```
void setup()

{

   Serial.begin(9600);      // opens serial port, sets data rate to 9600 bps

   lcd.begin(16, 2);    //// set up the LCD's number of
```

columns and rows:

```
pinMode(A0,OUTPUT);

pinMode(A1,OUTPUT);

pinMode(A2,OUTPUT);

pinMode(A3,OUTPUT);

pinMode(A4,INPUT);

lcd.print("Voltage Level");
}
```

Here, we make a capacity for utilizing the LED visual diagram to use in a straightforward way, you can even gleam the LEDs by programming them individually , yet the code get protracted.

```
void LED_function(int stage)

{

    for (int j=2; j<=11; j++)

    {
```

```
    digitalWrite(j,LOW);

}

for (int i=1, l=2; i<=stage; i++,l++)

{

    digitalWrite(l,HIGH);

    //delay(30);

}

}
```

In this part, we have perused the voltage worth utilizing the simple stick. At that point, we are changing over the simple incentive into a computerized voltage esteem by utilizing the simple to advanced transformation recipe and showing it further on LCD.

```
// Conversion formula for voltage

    analogValue = analogRead (A4);

    Serial.println(analogValue);

    delay (1000);
```

```
input_voltage = (analogValue * 5.0) / 1024.0;

lcd.setCursor(0, 1);

lcd.print("Voltage= ");

lcd.print(input_voltage);

Serial.println(input_voltage);

delay(100);
```

As indicated by the estimation of the info voltage we have given some condition to control the LED structured presentation LEDs. The condition you can check underneath in the code:

```
if (input_voltage < 0.50 && input_voltage >= 0.00 )

{

digitalWrite(2, HIGH);

delay (30);

digitalWrite(2, LOW);

delay (30);    // when the voltage is zero or low the
1st LED will indicate by blinking
```

```
}

else if (input_voltage < 1.00 && input_voltage >=
0.50)

{

LED_function(2);

}

else if (input_voltage < 1.50 && input_voltage >=
1.00)

{

LED_function(3);

}

else if (input_voltage < 2.00 && input_voltage >=
1.50)

{

LED_function(4);

}

else if (input_voltage < 2.50 && input_voltage >=
```

```
2.00)

{

LED_function(5);

}

else if (input_voltage < 3.00 && input_voltage >=
2.50)

{

LED_function(6);

}

else if (input_voltage < 3.50 && input_voltage >=
3.00)

{

LED_function(7);

}

else if (input_voltage < 4.00 && input_voltage >=
3.50)

{
```

```
LED_function(8);

}

else if (input_voltage < 4.50 && input_voltage >=
4.00)

{

LED_function(9);

}

else if (input_voltage < 5.00 && input_voltage >=
4.50)

{

LED_function(10);

}

}
```

Working of Battery Voltage Indicator

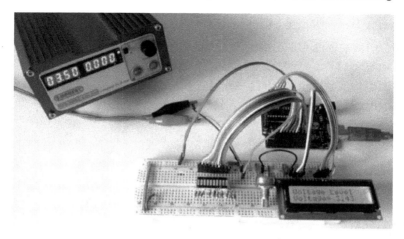

Battery Voltage Indicator simply read the incentive from Arduino Analog stick and convert it into a computerized an incentive by utilizing the ADC equation. The Arduino Uno ADC is of 10-piece goals (so the whole number qualities from 0 - 2^10 = 1024 qualities). This implies it will guide input voltages somewhere in the range of 0 and 5 volts into whole number qualities somewhere in the range of 0 and 1023. So in the event that we increase input anlogValue to (5/1024), at that point we get the advanced estimation of information voltage. Learn here how to utilize ADC contribution to Arduino. At that point the computerized worth is utilized to shine the LED reference chart in like manner.

Additionally, check this basic Battery level Monitor with no Microcontroller
Code

```
#include <LiquidCrystal.h>
const int rs = 12, en = 13, d0 = A0, d1 = A1, d2 = A2, d3
= A3;
LiquidCrystal lcd(rs, en, d0, d1, d2, d3);
const int analogPin = A4;
float analogValue;
float input_voltage;
int ledPins[] = {
2, 3, 4, 5, 6, 7, 8, 9, 10, 11
};        // an array of pin numbers to which LEDs are
attached
int pinCount = 10;        // the number of pins (i.e. the
length of the array)
void setup()
{
  Serial.begin(9600);    // opens serial port, sets data
rate to 9600 bps
  lcd.begin(16, 2);      //// set up the LCD's number of
columns and rows:
  pinMode(A0,OUTPUT);
  pinMode(A1,OUTPUT);
  pinMode(A2,OUTPUT);
  pinMode(A3,OUTPUT);
  pinMode(A4,INPUT);
  lcd.print("Voltage Level");
}
void LED_function(int stage)
{
  for (int j=2; j<=11; j++)
  {
```

```
digitalWrite(j,LOW);
}
for (int i=1, l=2; i<=stage; i++,l++)
{
digitalWrite(l,HIGH);
//delay(30);
}


}
void loop()
{
// Conversion formula for voltage
  analogValue = analogRead (A4);
  Serial.println(analogValue);
  delay (1000);
  input_voltage = (analogValue * 5.0) / 1024.0;
  lcd.setCursor(0, 1);
  lcd.print("Voltage= ");
  lcd.print(input_voltage);
  Serial.println(input_voltage);
  delay(100);
if (input_voltage < 0.50 && input_voltage >= 0.00 )
{
digitalWrite(2, HIGH);
delay (30);
digitalWrite(2, LOW);
delay (30);
}
else if (input_voltage < 1.00 && input_voltage >= 0.50)
```

```
{
LED_function(2);
}
else if (input_voltage < 1.50 && input_voltage >=
1.00)
{
LED_function(3);
}
else if (input_voltage < 2.00 && input_voltage >=
1.50)
{
LED_function(4);
}
else if (input_voltage < 2.50 && input_voltage >=
2.00)
{
LED_function(5);
}
else if (input_voltage < 3.00 && input_voltage >=
2.50)
{
LED_function(6);
}
else if (input_voltage < 3.50 && input_voltage >=
3.00)
{
LED_function(7);
}
else if (input_voltage < 4.00 && input_voltage >=
3.50)
{
```

```
LED_function(8);
}
else if (input_voltage < 4.50 && input_voltage >=
4.00)
{
LED_function(9);
}
else if (input_voltage < 5.00 && input_voltage >=
4.50)
{
LED_function(10);
}
}
```

2.LED BINARY CLOCK CIRCUIT USING ARDUINO

In this undertaking, we are gonna to make a LED Binary Clock Using Arduino. Here we have planned a printed circuit load up (PCB) to execute this clock. To plan PCB format, we have utilized EasyEDA online PCB structuring device.

Components Required:

- Arduino Nano
- 32.768Khz Crystal
- DS1307 RTC
- Resistor 1k, 10k
- 3v coin cell
- LEDs
- Power Supply

Circuit Diagram and Explanation:

Anbazhagan K

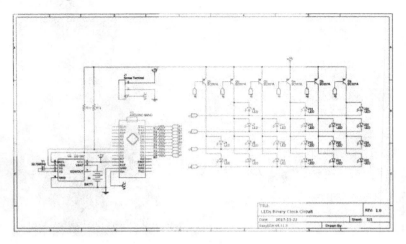

This is exceptionally straightforward, modest and intriguing undertaking for the student. In this LED Binary Clock Circuit, we have utilized Arduino Nano to control the entire undertaking like perusing time from RTC and demonstrating that on LEDs. A 3.0v coin cell is associated with RTC IC for reinforcement. Become familiar with utilizing DS1307 RTC with Arduino here.

20 LEDs are associated here in lattice structure. So here we have 6 segments and 4 lines. 2 sections utilized for demonstrating hour, next two segments for quite a long time and by segments for a considerable length of time. We have utilized 6 PNP transistor to triggers LEDs in 6 segments. The client can control the entire circuit by 5v just, here we have utilized PC USB for power supply. Rest of associations are appeared in circuit graph.

26

Further, check the total Arduino Code toward the finish of this Article.

How to Calculate and Read Time in Binary Clock:

As we know about parallel numbers that are zero and one. So by utilizing these, we can show time and we can change over that parallel time into the decimal. By utilizing the number 8 4 2 1 (composed on the Right half of PCB), we can change over double to decimal.

Assume we have a double number like:

1 0 1 0 so it will be 10 in decimal. When we convert double to decimal we just include ones.

Here from MSB (Most critical piece) side, we have 1 it implies 8 and next is 0 implies that is 0 and not to be incorporated. Next is again 1 methods 2 and the latter is 0 so the last one will likewise not be incorporated.

So at long last we have

8+0+2+0=10

Essentially, we can take it like this:

8x1 + 4x0 + 2x1 + 1x0 = 10

Presently we can comprehend time from the image:

In above, we can see there are 6 segments and 4 column. In these, we have 2 sections bunch HH for Hour, MM for Minute and SS for a considerable length of time. At the correct side of PCB, we can see column numbers 1, 2, 4, and 8, these numbers are utilized for changing over paired number to decimal

Note we are perusing sections from Right-Hand side. So as a matter of first importance, see HH sections, there are two segments of time. In the primary segment of time, there is no driven is gleaming methods:

2x0 + 1x0 = 0

In next section, we can see there is single driven is gleaming in the 1-push implies. So as per 8 4 2 1

8x0 + 4x0 + 2x0 + 1x1 = 1

So in Hour HH segment, we got 01.

In the main section of MM (minutes), we can see there is single driven is gleaming in the 1-push implies

4 2 1

4x0 + 2x0 + 1x1 = 1

In the second section of MM, we can see there is single driven is sparkling in the column number 8 methods

8 4 2 1

$$8 \times 1 + 4 \times 0 + 2 \times 0 + 1 \times 0 = 8$$

So we got minute as 18

In the primary section of SS (seconds), we can see there is single driven is shining in the line number 4 methods

4 2 1

$$4 \times 1 + 2 \times 0 + 1 \times 0 = 4$$

In the second segment of SS, we can see there is two driven is shining in the column number 1 and line number 4 methods

8 4 2 1

$$8 \times 0 + 4 \times 1 + 2 \times 0 + 1 \times 1 = 5$$

So we got minute as 45

So at long last we have time as 01:18:45

HH	MM	SS
01	18	45

Complete Arduino Code is given toward the finish of this Article.

Circuit and PCB Design using EasyEDA:

To plan this LED Binary Clock Circuit, we have picked the online EDA instrument called EasyEDA. I have recently utilized EasyEDA commonly and thought that it was exceptionally advantageous to use since it has a decent accumulation of impressions and its opensource. Check here our everything the PCB ventures. In the wake of planning the PCB, we can arrange the PCB tests by their minimal effort . They additionally offer part sourcing administration where they have a huge load of electronic segments and clients can arrange their required segments alongside the PCB request.

While structuring your circuits and PCBs, you can likewise make your circuit and PCB plans open with the goal that different clients can duplicate or alter them and can take profit by there, we have additionally made our entire Circuit and PCB designs open for this Arduino Binary Clock:

You can see any Layer (Top, Bottom, Topsilk, bottomsilk and so forth) of the PCB by choosing the layer structure the 'Layers' Window.

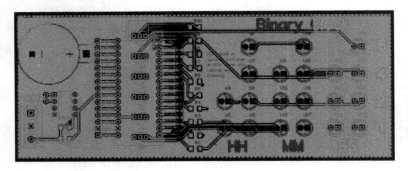

You can likewise see the PCB, how it will care for creation utilizing the Photo View catch in EasyEDA:

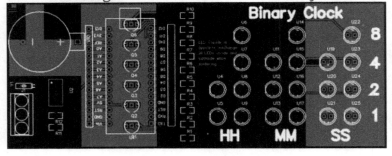

Calculating and Ordering Samples online:

In the wake of finishing the plan of this Arduino Binary Clock PCB, you can arrange the PCB through . To arrange the PCB from JLCPCB, you need Gerber File. To download Gerber documents of your PCB simply click the Fabrication Output catch in EasyEDA manager page, at that point download from the EasyEDA PCB request page.

Presently go to and click on Quote Now or Buy Now

catch, at that point you can choose the quantity of PCBs you need to arrange, what number of copper layers you need, the PCB thickness, copper weight, and even the PCB shading, similar to the preview demonstrated as follows:

After you have chosen the majority of the choices, click "Spare to Cart" and afterward you will be taken to the page where you can transfer your Gerber File which we have downloaded from EasyEDA. Transfer your Gerber record and snap "Spare to Cart". Lastly click on Checkout Securely to finish your request, at that point you will get your PCBs a few days after the fact. They are manufacturing the PCB at low rate which is $2. Their assemble time is additionally extremely less which is 48 hours with DHL conveyance of 3-5 days, essentially you will get your PCBs inside seven days of requesting.

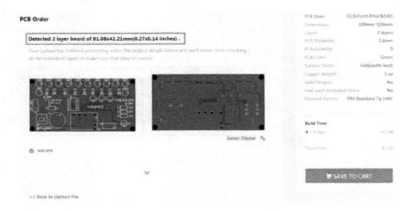

Following couple of long periods of requesting PCB's I got the PCB tests in pleasant bundling as appeared in underneath pictures.

Also, in the wake of getting these pieces I have welded all the required parts over the PCB, put the coded Arduino Nano and controlled it with 5v supply to see the Binary Clock in real life.

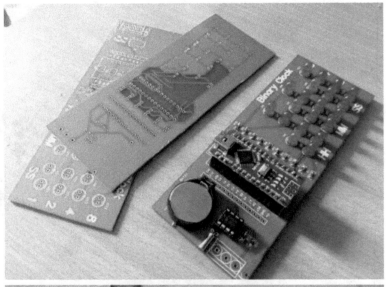

Code

```
#include <Wire.h>
#include "RTClib.h"
#include <TimerOne.h>
RTC_DS1307 RTC;
int temp,inc,hours1,minut,add=11;
#define d1 12
#define d2 11
#define d3 10
#define d4 9
#define d5 8
#define d6 7
#define r1 6
#define r2 5
#define r3 4
#define r4 3
int HOUR,MINUT,SECOND;
volatile int count=0;
void Clear(int d)
{
  digitalWrite(d1, HIGH);
  digitalWrite(d2, HIGH);
  digitalWrite(d3, HIGH);
  digitalWrite(d4, HIGH);
  digitalWrite(d5, HIGH);
  digitalWrite(d6, HIGH);
}
void callback()
```

```
{
digitalWrite(13, digitalRead(13) ^ 1);
count++;
if(count>=7)
count=1;
switch(count%7)
{
 case 1:
 Clear(d1);
 temp=SECOND%10;
 show(temp);
 digitalWrite(d1, LOW);
 break;

 case 2:
 Clear(d2);
 temp=SECOND/10;
 show(temp);
 digitalWrite(d2, LOW);
 for(int i=0;i<10000;i++)
 {
 }
 break;


  case 3:
 Clear(d3);
 temp=MINUT%10;
 show(temp);
 digitalWrite(d3, LOW);
 for(int i=0;i<10000;i++)
 {
```

```
}
break;
case 4:
Clear(d4);
temp=MINUT/10;
show(temp);
digitalWrite(d4,LOW);
for(int i=0;i<10000;i++)
{
}
break;
case 5:
Clear(d5);
temp=HOUR%10;
show(temp);
digitalWrite(d5,LOW);
for(int i=0;i<10000;i++)
{
}
break;
case 6:
Clear(d6);
temp=HOUR/10;
show(temp);
digitalWrite(d6,LOW);
for(int i=0;i<10000;i++)
{
}
break;
}
```

```
}
void show(int d)
{
  for(int i=0;i<1;i++)
  {
   digitalWrite(r4,!((temp>>0)&1));
   digitalWrite(r3,!((temp>>1)&1));
   digitalWrite(r2,!((temp>>2)&1));
   digitalWrite(r1,!((temp>>3)&1));
   // delay(1);
   for(int i=0;i<1000;i++);
  }
}


void setup()
{
Wire.begin();
Serial.begin(9600);
RTC.begin();
digitalWrite(next, HIGH);
digitalWrite(set_mad, HIGH);
digitalWrite(INC, HIGH);
pinMode(14, OUTPUT);
for(int i=2;i<=12;i++)
{
pinMode(i, OUTPUT);
 digitalWrite(i, HIGH);
}
```

```
if(!RTC.isrunning())
{
RTC.adjust(DateTime(__DATE__,__TIME__));
}
Timer1.initialize(1000);
Timer1.attachInterrupt(callback);
}

void loop()
{
int temp=0,val=1,temp4;
DateTime now = RTC.now();
HOUR=now.hour();
MINUT=now.minute();
SECOND=now.second();
Serial.print(HOUR);
Serial.print(":");
Serial.print(MINUT);
Serial.print(":");
Serial.println(SECOND);
delay(200);
}
```

3.MEASURING PPM FROM MQ GAS SENSORS USING ARDUINO (MQ-137 AMMONIA)

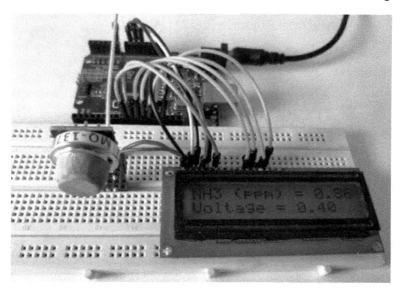

Directly from the hour of modern age, we humanity have been quickly creating. With each progress we additionally dirty our condition and inevitably corrupting it. Presently an unnatural weather change is a disturbing danger and even the air that we inhale are getting basic. So air quality observing has likewise begun to pick up significance. So in this article we will find out how to utilize any MQ arrangement gas sensor with Arduino and demonstrating the yield in PPM . PPM is additionally communicated as (mg/L). These sensors are normally accessible and are likewise solid for estimating various sorts of gas demonstrated as follows

MQ-series Gas sensors

- Carbon Dioxide (CO2) : MG-811

- Carbon Monoxide (CO): MQ-9

- Absolute Volatile Organic Compounds (TVOCs): CCS811

- Comparable Carbon Dioxide (eCO2): CCS811

- Metal Oxide (MOX): CCS811

- Smelling salts: MQ-137

- Air Quality: MQ-135

- LPG, Alcohol, Smoke: MQ2

We have just utilized MQ2 for smoke detecting and MQ-135 for Air quality checking venture. Here I will utilize the MQ-137 sensor from sainsmart to gauge smelling salts in ppm. With the sensor close by I experienced all the accessible instructional exercises and found that there has no appropriate documentation on the most proficient method to quantify the gas in ppm. Most instructional exercises either manage just the Analog qualities or present a few constants which are not dependable for estimating all kind of gas. So in the wake of fiddling around online for quite a while I at last discovered how to utilize these MQ arrangement gas sensors to quantify ppm utilizing Arduino. I am clarifying things from the base with no libraries so you can utilize this article for any Gas sensor accessible with you.

Preparing your Hardware:

The MQ gas sensors can either obtained as a module or similarly as a sensor alone. On the off chance that your motivation is to quantify just ppm, at that point it's ideal to purchase the sensor alone since the module is useful for just utilizing the Digital stick. So in the event that you have bought the module effectively, at that point you need to play out a little hack which will be talked about further. For the time being, we should accept you have bought the sensor. The pinout and association of the sensor is demonstrated as follows

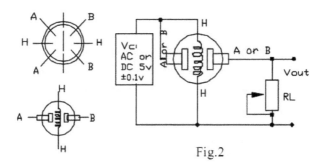

Fig.2

As should be obvious you simply need to interface one finish of 'H' to supply and the opposite finish of 'H' to ground. At that point join both An's and both B's. Interface one set to supply voltage and the other to your simple stick. The resistor RL assumes a significant job in making the sensor work. So make a note of which worth you are utilizing, an estimation of 47k is suggested.

On the off chance that you have just obtained a module, at that point you should follow your PCB follows to discover the estimation of your RL in the board. Grauonline has just done this work for us as well as the circuit graph of the MQ gas sensor board is given beneath.

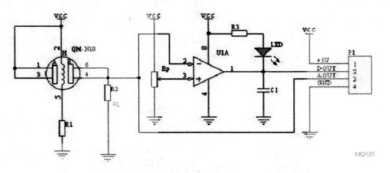

As should be obvious the resistor RL (R2) is associated between the Aout stick and the ground, so on the off chance that you are having a module the estimation of RL can be estimated by utilizing a multimeter in opposition mode crosswise over Vout stick and Vcc stick of the module. In my sainsmart MQ-137 gas sensor the estimation of RL was 1K and was situated here as appeared in the image underneath.

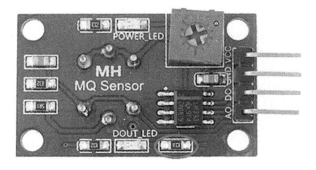

In any case, the site guarantees that it gives a variable pot of RL which isn't valid as you can unmistakably find in the circuit chart, the pot is utilized to set the variable voltage for operation amp as well as having nothing to do with RL. So we need to physically weld the SMD resistor (1K) appeared above and we need to utilize our own resistor over the Ground and Vout stick which will go about as RL. The best an incentive for RL will be 47K as proposed by datasheet subsequently we are going to utilize the equivalent.

Approach to Measure PPM from MQ Gas Sensors:

Since we know the estimation of RL lets continue on the most proficient method to really gauge ppm from these sensors. Like all sensors the spot to begin is its datasheet. The MQ-137 Datasheet is shown here yet ensure you locate the right datasheet for your sensor. Inside the datasheet we are need just one chart which will be plotted against (Rs/Ro) VS PPM this is the one that we requirement for our figurings. So chatter it and keep it somewhere convenient. The one for my sensor is demonstrated as follows.

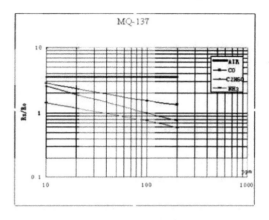

Fig.3 is shows the typical sensitivity characteristics of the MQ-137 for several gases. in their: Temp: 20℃ , Humidity: 65% . O₂ concentration 21% RL=47k Ω
Ro: sensor resistance in the clean air.
Rs :sensor resistance at various concentrations of gases.

Fig 3 sensitivity characteristics of the MQ-137

Turns out that MQ137 sensor can gauge NH3, C2H6O and even CO. Be that as it may, here I am intrigued distinctly with regards to the estimations of NH3. Anyway you can utilize a similar strategy to compute ppm for any sensor you like. This chart is the main hotspot for us to discover the estimation of ppm and on the off chance that we could by in some way compute the proportion of Rs/Ro (X-hub) we can utilize this diagram to discover the estimation of ppm (Y-hub). To discover the estimation of Rs/Ro we have to discover the estimation of Rs and the estimation of Ro. Where Rs is the Sensor opposition at gas focus as well as Ro is the sensor obstruction in clean sir.

Yess... this is the arrangement how about we perceive how we can pull off this....

Calculating the Value of Ro at Clean Air:

Note that in the diagram estimation of Rs/Ro is steady for air (thick blue line) so we can utilize this furthering our potential benefit and state that when the sensor is working in natural air the estimation of Rs/Ro will be 3.6 allude the image beneath

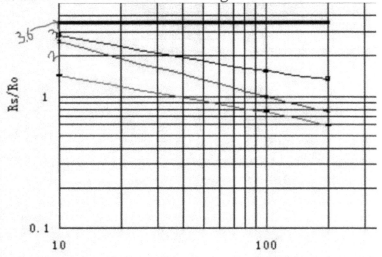

Rs/Ro = 3.6

From the datasheet we likewise get the opportunity to have an equation for ascertaining the estimation of Rs. The equation is demonstrated as follows. In the event that you are intrigued to know how this equation is inferred you can peruse jay con frameworks, I might likewise want to credit them in bailing me to deal with this.

Resistance of sensor(Rs): Rs=(Vc/VRL-1)×RL

In this equation the estimation of Vc is our inventory voltage (+5V) and the estimation of RL is the one that we determined effectively (47K for my sensor). In the event that we compose a little Arduino program we could likewise discover the estimation of VRL lastly figure the estimation of Rs. I have given an Arduino Program beneath which peruses the simple voltage (VRL) of the sensor and ascertains the estimation of Rs utilizing this recipe lastly shows it in the sequential screen. The program is all around clarified through the remark segment so I am avoiding its clarification here in order to keep this article short.

```
//This program works best at a fresh air room with
temperaure Temp: 20°C, Humidity: 65%, O2 con-
centration 21% and when the value of Rl is 47K

#define RL 47  //The value of resistor RL is 47K

void setup() //Runs only once

{

  Serial.begin(9600); //Initialise serial COM for dis-
playing the value

}
```

```
void loop() {

    float analog_value;

    float VRL;

    float Rs;

    float Ro;

    for(int test_cycle = 1 ; test_cycle <= 500 ; test_
    cycle++) //Read the analog output of the sensor for
    200 times

    {

        analog_value   =   analog_value   +   analo-
        gRead(A0); //add the values for 200

    }

    analog_value = analog_value/500.0; //Take aver-
    age

    VRL = analog_value*(5.0/1023.0); //Convert ana-
    log value to voltage

    //RS = ((Vc/VRL)-1)*RL is the formulae we ob-
    tained from datasheet
```

```
Rs = ((5.0/VRL)-1)*RL;

//RS/RO is 3.6 as we obtained from graph of da-
tasheet

Ro = Rs/3.6;

Serial.print("Ro at fresh air = ");

Serial.println(Ro); //Display calculated Ro

delay(1000); //delay of 1 sec
}
```

Note: The estimation of Ro will change, enable the sensor to pre-heat in any event for 10 hours and afterward utilize the estimation of Ro.

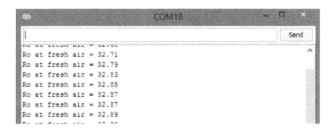

I closed the estimation of Ro to be 30K? for my sensor (when RL is 47k?). Yours strength somewhat shift.

Measure the value of Rs:

Since we know the estimation of Ro we can without much of a stretch compute the estimation of Rs utilizing the over two formulae. Note that the estimation of Rs that was determined already is for outside cool and it won't be a similar when smelling salts is available noticeable all around. Figuring the estimation of Rs is anything but a major issue which we can legitimately take care in the last program.

Relating Rs/Ro ratio with PPM:

Since we realize how to quantify the estimation of Rs and Ro we would have the option to discover its proportion (Rs/Ro). At that point we can utilize the graph (demonstrated as follows) to identify with the comparing estimation of PPM.

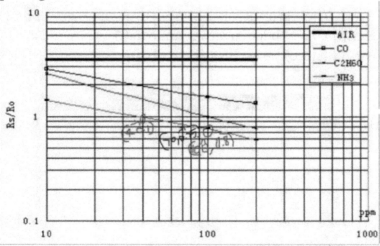

In spite of the fact that the NH3 line (cyan shading)

seems, by all accounts, to be straight it is really not direct. The appearance is on the grounds that the scale is partitioned un-consistently for appearance. So the relating between Rs/Ro and PPM is really logarithmic which can be spoken to by the underneath condition.

$$\log(y) = m^*\log(x) + b$$

where,

y = ratio (Rs/Ro)

x = PPM

m = slope of the line

b = intersection point

To discover the estimations of m and b we need to think about two points (x1,y1) as well as (x2,y2) on our gas line. Here we are working with alkali so the two I have considered is (40,1) and (100,0.8) as appeared in the image above (set apart as red) with red checking.

$$m = [\log(y2) - \log(y1)] / [\log(x2) - \log(x1)]$$

$$m = \log(0.8/1) / \log(100/40)$$

$$m = -0.243$$

So also for (b) we should get the midpoint esteem (x,y) from the diagram which is (70,0.75) as appeared in picture above (set apart in blue)

$$b = \log(y) - m^*\log(x)$$

$$b = \log(0.75) - (-0.243)^*\log(70)$$

$$b = 0.323$$

That is it since we have determined the estimation of m and b we can liken the estimation of (Rs/Ro) to PPM utilizing the underneath equation

$$PPM = 10 \wedge \{[\log(ratio) - b] / m\}$$

Program to calculate PPM using MQ sensor:

The total program to ascertain PPM utilizing a MQ sensor is given beneath. Barely any significant lines are clarified beneath.

Before continuing with the program we have to nourish in the estimations of Load obstruction (RL),

Slope(m), Intercept(b) and the estimation of Resistance in outside air (Ro). The methodology to acquire every one of these qualities have as of now be clarified so allows simply feed them in now

```
#define RL 47 //The value of resistor RL is 47K

#define m -0.263 //Enter calculated Slope

#define b 0.42 //Enter calculated intercept

#define Ro 30 //Enter found Ro value
```

At that point read the Voltage drop over the sensor (VRL) as well as convert it to Voltage (0V to 5V) from the simple read will just return esteems from 0 to 1024.

```
VRL = analogRead(MQ_sensor)*(5.0/1023.0); // Measure the voltage drop and convert to 0-5V
```

Presently, that the estimation of VRL is determined you can utilize the recipe examined above to ascertain the estimation of Rs and the additionally the proportion (Rs/Ro)

```
ratio = Rs/Ro; // find ratio Rs/Ro
```

At last, we can ascertain the PPM with our logarithmic equation and show it on our sequential screen as demonstrated as follows

```
double ppm = pow(10, ((log10(ratio)-b)/m)); //use
formula to calculate ppm

Serial.print(ppm); //Display ppm
```

Showing PPM value on Hardware with Arduino and MQ-137:

Enough of all the hypothesis let us manufacture a basic circuit with the sensor and LCD to show the estimation of gas in PPM. Here the sensor I am utilizing is MQ137 which estimates smelling salts, the circuit outline for my set up is demonstrated as follows.

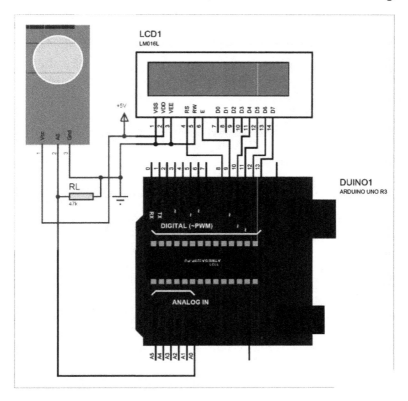

Interface your sensor and your LCD as appeared in the Circuit chart and transfer the code given toward the finish of the program. You need to alter the Ro esteem as clarified previously. Additionally roll out the improvements in parameter esteems in the event that you are utilizing some other resistor as RL other than 4.7K.

Leave your set-up fueled for at any rate 2 hours before you take any readings, (48 hrs is suggested for increasingly exact qualities). This time is known as the warming time, during which the sensor heats up. After this, you ought to have the option to see the estimation of PPM and the voltage showed on your LCD screen as demonstrated as follows.

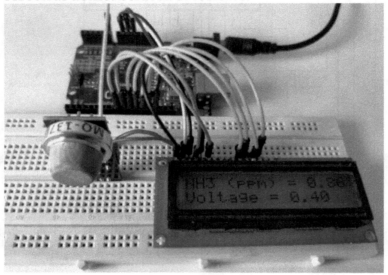

Presently to guarantee if the qualities are truly identified with the nearness of smelling salts, how about we place this set-up inside a shut compartment and send alkali gas inside it to check if the qualities are expanding. I don't have an appropriate PPM meter with me adjust it and it would extraordinary in the event that somebody with meter could test this set-up and let me know.

Code

```
#define RL 47 //The value of resistor RL is 47K
#define m -0.263 //Enter calculated Slope
#define b 0.42 //Enter calculated intercept
#define Ro 20 //Enter found Ro value
#define MQ_sensor A0 //Sensor is connected to A4
#include <LiquidCrystal.h> //Header file for
LCD from https://www.arduino.cc/en/Reference/
LiquidCrystal
const int rs = 8, en = 9, d4 = 10, d5 = 11, d6 = 12, d7 =
13; //Pins to which LCD is connected
LiquidCrystal lcd(rs, en, d4, d5, d6, d7);
void setup() {
 lcd.begin(16, 2); //We are using a 16*2 LCD display
 lcd.print("NH3 in PPM"); //Display a intro message
 lcd.setCursor(0, 1);   // set the cursor to column 0,
line 1
 lcd.print("-Hello_world"); //Display a intro message
 delay(2000); //Wait for display to show info
 lcd.clear(); //Then clean it
}
void loop() {
 float VRL; //Voltage drop across the MQ sensor
 float Rs; //Sensor resistance at gas concentration
 float ratio; //Define variable for ratio
```

```
VRL = analogRead(MQ_sensor)*(5.0/1023.0); //
Measure the voltage drop and convert to 0-5V
Rs = ((5.0*RL)/VRL)-RL; //Use formula to get Rs value
ratio = Rs/Ro; // find ratio Rs/Ro


float ppm = pow(10,((log10(ratio)-b)/m)); //use for-
mula to calculate ppm
lcd.print("NH3 (ppm) = "); //Display a ammonia in
ppm
lcd.print(ppm);
lcd.setCursor(0, 1);   // set the cursor to column 0,
line 1
lcd.print("Voltage = "); //Display a intro message
lcd.print(VRL);
delay(200);
lcd.clear(); //Then clean it
}
```

4.ARDUINO CALCULATOR USING 4X4 KEYPAD

Writing computer programs is constantly fun and Arduino is an awesome stage in the event that you are simply beginning with Embedded programming. In this instructional exercise we will manufacture our own adding machine with Arduino. The qualities can be sent in through a keypad (4×4 keypad) and result can be seen on a LCD screen (16×2 Dot-framework). This mini-computer could perform basic activities like +, - , (*)as well as(/)with entire numbers. Nethertheless, when you comprehend the idea you can actualize even logical capacities with Arduino's worked in capacities.

Toward the finish of this undertaking you will realize how to utilize a 16x2 LCD and Keypad with Arduino and furthermore that it is so natural to program for them utilizing the promptly accessible libraries. You will likewise see how to program your Arduino for achieving a specific undertaking.

Materials Required:

- Breadboard

- 16×2 LCD Display

- Arduino Uno (Any adaptation will work)

- 9V Battery

- 4×4 Keypad

- Interfacing wires

Circuit Diagram:

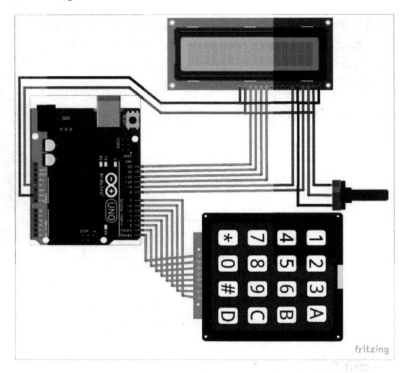

The total circuit chart of this Arduino Calculator Project is given above. The +5V and ground association appeared in the circuit outline can be acquired from the 5V and ground stick of the Arduino. The Arduino itself can be fueled from your workstation or through the DC jack utilizing a 12V connector or 9V battery.

We are working the LCD in 4-piece mode with Arduino so just the last four information bits of the LCD is associated with Arduino. The Keyboard will have 8 yield pins which must be associated from stick 0 to stick 7 as appeared previously. You can utilize the accompanying association table to confirm your association with Arduino, you can likewise check 4x4 Keypad interfacing with Arduino.

Arduino Pin Name:	Connected to:
D0	1st pin of the keyboard
D1	2nd pin of the keyboard
D2	3rd pin of the keyboard
D3	4th pin of the keyboard
D4	5th pin of the keyboard
D5	6th pin of the keyboard
D6	7th pin of the keyboard
D7	8th pin of the keyboard
D8	Register select pin of LCD (pin 4)
D9	Enable pin of LCD (pin 6)
D10	Data pin 4 (pin 11)
D11	Data pin 4 (pin 11)
D12	Data pin 4 (pin 11)
D13	Data pin 4 (pin 11)
+5V	Connected to Vdd pin of LCD (pin 2)

Ground	Connected to Vss,Vee and RW pin of LCD (pin 1,3 and 5)

Some Arduino sheets may demonstrate a blunder while transferring program if there are anything associated with stick 0 and pin1, so on the off chance that you experience any simply expel the keypad while transferring the program.

When your associations are done your equipment will look something like this underneath

Arduino Calculator Program:

The total Arduino program for this venture is given toward the finish of this undertaking. The code is part into little significant pieces and clarified underneath.

As advised before we are gonna to interface a LCD as well as keypad with Arduino utilizing libraries. So how about we add them to our Arduino IDE first. The library for LCD is as of now incorporated into your Arduino of course so we need not stress over it. For Keypad library click on the connection to download it from Github. You will get a ZIP document, at that point add this lib to Arduino by Sketch - > Include Library - > Add .ZIP record and indicate the area this downloaded record. When done we are good to go for programming.

Despite the fact that we have utilized a library for utilizing a keypad we need to make reference to few subtleties (demonstrated as follows) about the keypad to the Arduino. The variable ROWS and COLS will tell what number of lines and sections our keypad has and the keymap demonstrates the request where the keys are available on the console. The keypad that I am utilizing in this venture resembles this beneath to the key guide additionally speaks to the equivalent.

Further beneath we have referenced to which sticks the Keypad is associated utilizing the variable cluster rowPins and colPins.

```
const byte ROWS = 4; // Four rows

const byte COLS = 4; // Three columns

// Define the Keymap

char keys[ROWS][COLS] = {

  {'1','2','3','A'},

  {'4','5','6','B'},

  {'7','8','9','C'},

  {'*','0','#','D'}

};

byte rowPins[ROWS] = { 0, 1, 2, 3 };// Connect keypad ROW0, ROW1, ROW2 and ROW3 to these Arduino pins.

byte colPins[COLS] = { 4, 5, 6, 7 }; // Connect keypad COL0, COL1 and COL2 to these Arduino pins.
```

When we have referenced what sort of keypad we are utilizing and how it is associated, we can make the keypad utilizing those subtleties utilizing the line beneath

```
Keypad kpd = Keypad( makeKeymap(keys), row-
Pins, colPins, ROWS, COLS ); // Create the Keypad
```

Essentially we additionally need to advise to which pins of the Arduino the LCD is associated with. As indicated by our circuit outline the definitions would resemble beneath

```
const int rs = 8, en = 9, d4 = 10, d5 = 11, d6 = 12, d7 =
13; //Pins to which LCD is connected

LiquidCrystal lcd(rs, en, d4, d5, d6, d7); //create the
LCD
```

Inside the arrangement work, we simply show the name of the venture and afterward continue to while circle where the principle undertaking lies.

Fundamentally, we need to check in the event that anything is being composed on the keypad, whenever composed we need to perceive what is being composed and after that convert it to a variable when the "=" is squeezed we need to compute the outcome and afterward at long last show it on the LCD. This is actually what is done inside the circle work as demonstrated as follows

```
key = kpd.getKey(); //storing pressed key value in a
char

if(key!=NO_KEY)

DetectButtons();

if(result==true)

CalculateResult();

DisplayResult();
```

What occurs inside each capacity is clarified utilizing the remark lines, experience the total code beneath, tinker with it to see how it really functions. In case you have any uncertainty on a particular line, don't hesitate to utilize the remark area or the gatherings.

Simulation of Arduino Calculator:

We can likewise have a go at mimicking the venture utilizing Proteus programming. Proteus doesn't have an Arduino segment alone, however can be effectively downloaded and added to its library. When you have the Arduino part on Proteus, simply add Alphanumeric LCD and Keypad to make the association as appeared in the circuit graph.

At that point download the hex record from here and add it to the Arduino by double tapping on board in Proteus and point the "program document" to this downloaded hex document. A depiction of the re-enactment is demonstrated as follows.

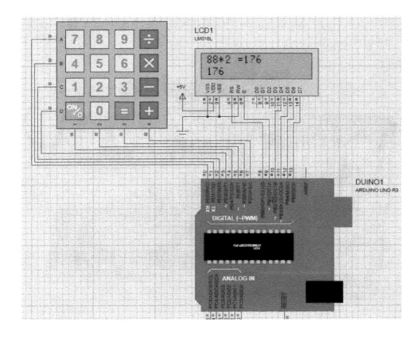

Note: The hex record given isn't as same as the first of the program given underneath. It has been adjusted to since the keymap of the recreation keypad and the real equipment keypad is extraordinary.

Working of Arduino Calculator:

Make the associations according to circuit chart and transfer the code beneath. In case it indicates mistake ensure you have included the library according to the guidance given above. You can likewise attempt the recreation to check if the issue is with your equipment. On the off chance that everything is done as it should be, at that point your equipment will look something like this underneath with the LCD showing this

Since the keypad utilized here doesn't have legitimate markings on it I have accepted the Alphabets to be administrators as recorded beneath

Character on Keypad	Assumed to be

Arduino best 10 measurement, Calculation and monitoring

"A"	Addition (+)
"B"	Subtraction (-)
"C"	Multiplication (*)
"D"	Division (/)
"*"	Clear (C)
"#"	Equals (=)

You can utilize a marker to compose over what each catch really speaks to.

With that done, you can straightforwardly begin utilizing the adding machine. Types the number and will show up on the subsequent line press the operand and type your subsequent number at last press the "#" key to get your outcome. You can likewise have a go at structure this Touchscreen based Arduino number cruncher.

Code

```
/*
* Arduino Keypad calculator Program
*/
#include <LiquidCrystal.h> //Header file for
LCD from https://www.arduino.cc/en/Reference/
LiquidCrystal
#include <Keypad.h> //Header file for Keypad
from https://github.com/Chris--A/Keypad
const byte ROWS = 4; // Four rows
```

```
const byte COLS = 4; // Three columns
// Define the Keymap
char keys[ROWS][COLS] = {
  {'7','8','9','D'},
  {'4','5','6','C'},
  {'1','2','3','B'},
  {'*','0','#','A'}
};
```

byte rowPins[ROWS] = { 0, 1, 2, 3 };// Connect keypad ROW0, ROW1, ROW2 and ROW3 to these Arduino pins.
byte colPins[COLS] = { 4, 5, 6, 7 }; // Connect keypad COL0, COL1 and COL2 to these Arduino pins.

Keypad kpd = Keypad(makeKeymap(keys), rowPins, colPins, ROWS, COLS); // Create the Keypad

const int rs = 8, en = 9, d4 = 10, d5 = 11, d6 = 12, d7 = 13; //Pins to which LCD is connected
LiquidCrystal lcd(rs, en, d4, d5, d6, d7);

long Num1,Num2,Number;
char key,action;
boolean result = false;

void setup() {
 lcd.begin(16, 2); //We are using a 16*2 LCD display
 lcd.print("DIY Calculator"); //Display a intro message
  lcd.setCursor(0, 1);   // set the cursor to column 0, line 1
 lcd.print("-Hello_world"); //Display a intro message
```
```

```
  delay(2000); //Wait for display to show info
  lcd.clear(); //Then clean it
}
void loop() {


key = kpd.getKey(); //storing pressed key value in a
char
if(key!=NO_KEY)
DetectButtons();
if(result==true)
CalculateResult();
DisplayResult();
}
void DetectButtons()
{
  lcd.clear(); //Then clean it
  if(key=='*') //If cancel Button is pressed
   {Serial.println ("Button Cancel"); Number=Num1=
Num2=0; result=false;}


   if(key == '1') //If Button 1 is pressed
  {Serial.println ("Button 1");
  if(Number==0)
  Number=1;
  else
  Number = (Number*10) + 1; //Pressed twice
  }
```

```
   if(key == '4') //If Button 4 is pressed
{Serial.println ("Button 4");
if(Number==0)
Number=4;
else
Number = (Number*10) + 4; //Pressed twice
}


   if(key == '7') //If Button 7 is pressed
{Serial.println ("Button 7");
if(Number==0)
Number=7;
else
Number = (Number*10) + 7; //Pressed twice
}


if(key == '0')
{Serial.println ("Button 0"); //Button 0 is Pressed
if(Number==0)
Number=0;
else
Number = (Number*10) + 0; //Pressed twice
}


   if(key == '2') //Button 2 is Pressed
{Serial.println ("Button 2");
 if(Number==0)
Number=2;
```

```
else
Number = (Number*10) + 2; //Pressed twice
}


   if(key == '5')
{Serial.println ("Button 5");
 if(Number==0)
Number=5;
else
Number = (Number*10) + 5; //Pressed twice
}


   if(key == '8')
{Serial.println ("Button 8");
 if(Number==0)
Number=8;
else
Number = (Number*10) + 8; //Pressed twice
}

if(key == '#')
{Serial.println ("Button Equal");
Num2=Number;
result = true;
}


   if(key == '3')
{Serial.println ("Button 3");
```

```
if(Number==0)
Number=3;
else
Number = (Number*10) + 3; //Pressed twice
}


   if(key == '6')
{Serial.println ("Button 6");
if(Number==0)
Number=6;
else
Number = (Number*10) + 6; //Pressed twice
}


   if(key == '9')
{Serial.println ("Button 9");
if(Number==0)
Number=9;
else
Number = (Number*10) + 9; //Pressed twice
}
   if (key == 'A' || key == 'B' || key == 'C' || key == 'D') //
Detecting Buttons on Column 4
{
Num1 = Number;
Number =0;
if(key == 'A')
{Serial.println ("Addition"); action = '+';}
   if(key == 'B')
```

```
  {Serial.println ("Subtraction"); action = '-';}
  if(key == 'C')
  {Serial.println ("Multiplication"); action = '*';}
  if(key == 'D')
  {Serial.println ("Devesion"); action = '/';}
  delay(100);
  }


}
void CalculateResult()
{
 if(action=='+')
  Number = Num1+Num2;
 if(action=='-')
  Number = Num1-Num2;
 if(action=='*')
  Number = Num1*Num2;
 if(action=='/')
  Number = Num1/Num2;
}
void DisplayResult()
{
  lcd.setCursor(0, 0);   // set the cursor to column 0,
line 1
     lcd.print(Num1);   lcd.print(action);   lcd.print(
Num2);


  if(result==true)
```

```
{lcd.print(" ="); lcd.print(Number);} //Display the re-
sult


  lcd.setCursor(0, 1);   // set the cursor to column 0,
line 1
  lcd.print(Number); //Display the result
}
```

5.SMART BLIND STICK USING ARDUINO

Have you ever known about Hugh Herr? He is a well known American shake climber who has broken the impediments of his inabilities; he is a solid devotee that innovation could help debilitated people to carry on with an ordinary life. In one of his TED talk Herr said "People are not impaired. An individual can never be broken. Our constructed condition, our advancements, is broken and crippled. We the individuals need not acknowledge our restrictions, yet can move inability through mechanical Innovation". These were words as well as he carried on with his life to them, today he utilizes Prosthetic legs and cases to live to ordinary life. So truly, innovation can for sure kill human inability; in light of this let us utilize the intensity of Arduino and basic sensors to fabricate a Blind man's stick that could perform something other than a stick for outwardly impeded people.

This Smart stick will have a Ultrasonic sensor to detect good ways from any hindrance, LDR to detect lighting conditions as well as a RF remote utilizing which the visually impaired man could remotely find his stick. Every one of the inputs will be given to the visually impaired man through a Buzzer. Obviously you can utilize a vibrator engine instead of Buzzer and advance much all the more utilizing your innovativeness.

Materials Required:

- Arduino Nano (Any version will work)
- LDR
- Buzzer and LED
- Ultrasonic Sensor HC-SR04
- 7805
- 433 MHz RF transmitter as well as receiver
- Resistors
- Push button
- Perf board
- Soldering Kit
- 9 V batteries

Circuit Diagram:

This Arduino Smart Blind Stick Project need 2 separate circuits. One is the primary circuit which will be mounted on the visually impaired man's stick. The other is a little remote RF transmitter circuit which will be utilized to find the fundamental circuit. The principle board's circuit chart is demonstrated as follows:

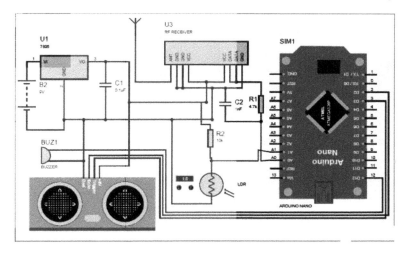

As should be obvious an Arduino Nano is utilized to control every one of the sensors. The total board is fueled by a 9V battery which is directed to +5V utilizing a 7805 Voltage controller. The Ultrasonic sensor is fueled by 5V as well as the trigger as well as Echo stick is associated with Arduino nano stick three as well as two as appeared previously. The LDR is associated with a resistor of significant worth 10K to frame a Potential divider and the distinction in voltage is perused by Arduino ADC stick A1. The ADC stick A0 is used to peruse the sign from RF collector. The yield of the board is given by the Buzzer which is associated with stick 12.

The RF remote circuit is demonstrated as follows. Its working is additionally clarified.

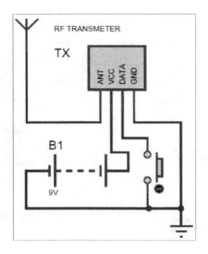

I have utilized a little hack to make this RF remote control circuit to work. Typically while utilizing this 433 MHz module requires an Encoder and Decoder or two MCU to work. However, in our application we simply need the recipient to recognize if the transmitter is sending a few sign. So the Data stick of the transmitter is associated with Ground or Vcc of the inventory.

The information stick of the recipient is gone through a RC channel and afterward given to the Arduino as demonstrated as follows. Presently, at whatever point the catch is squeezed the Receiver yield some steady ADC esteem over and over. This redundancy can't be seen when the catch isn't squeezed. So we compose the Arduino program to check for rehashed esteems to identify if the catch is squeezed. So that is the means by which a Blind individual can follow his stick. You can check here: how RF transmitter and collector work.

I have utilized a perf board to weld every one of the associations so it gets flawless with the stick. Be that as it may, you can likewise make them on a breadboard. The sheets that I made are beneath.

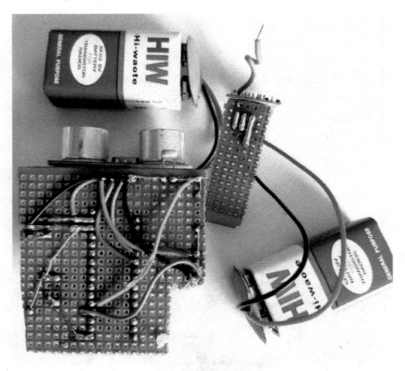

Arduino Program for Smart Blind Stick:

When we are prepared with our equipment, we can interface the Arduino to our Computer and start programming. The total code utilized for this page is at the base of this page, you can transfer it straightforwardly to your Arduino board. In any case, you are interested to know how the code functions read further.

Like all projects we begin with void arrangement() to start Input Output pins. In our program the Buzzer and Trigger stick is an Output gadget and the Echo stick is an Input gadget. We likewise initialise the sequential screen for investigating.

```
void setup()

{

Serial.begin(9600);

pinMode(Buzz,OUTPUT);

digitalWrite(Buzz,LOW);

pinMode(trigger, OUTPUT);

pinMode(echo, INPUT);

}
```

Inside the primary circle we are perusing every one of the sensors information. We start with perusing the sensor information of Ultrasonic sensor for separation, LDR for light force and RF sign to check if the catch is squeezed. Every information is spared in a variable as appeared beneath for sometime later.

```
calculate_distance(trigger,echo);
```

```
Signal = analogRead(Remote);

Intens = analogRead(Light);
```

We start with checking for the Remote sign. We utilize a variable called similar_count to check how often similar qualities are being rehashed from the RF beneficiary. This reiteration will happen just when the catch is squeezed. So we trigger the Remote squeezed caution if the check surpasses an estimation of 100.

```
//Check if Remote is pressed

int temp = analogRead(Remote);

similar_count=0;

while (Signal==temp)

{

Signal = analogRead(Remote);

 similar_count++;

}

//If remote pressed
```

```
if(similar_count<100)

{

    Serial.print(similar_count);    Serial.println("Re-
mote Pressed");

    digitalWrite(Buzz,HIGH);delay(3000);digital-
Write(Buzz,LOW);

}
```

You can likewise check it on Serial Monitor on your PC:

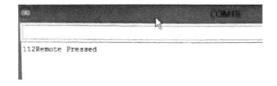

Next we check for the power of light around the visually impaired man. In the event that the LDR gives an estimation of under 200 it is thought to be exceptionally dim and we give him the notice through bell with a particular tone of postponement with 200ms.In case the power is brilliant that is more than 800, at that point additionally we give a notice with another tone. The caution tone and force can be effectively shifted by changing the particular incentive in the beneath code.

```
//If very dark

if(Intens<200)

{

  Serial.print(Intens); Serial.println("Bright Light");

  digitalWrite(Buzz,HIGH);delay(200);digital-
Write(Buzz,LOW);delay(200);digitalWrite(
Buzz,HIGH);delay(200);digitalWrite(
Buzz,LOW);delay(200);

  delay(500);

}

//If very bright

if(Intens>800)

{

  Serial.print(Intens); Serial.println("Low Light");

  digitalWrite(Buzz,HIGH);delay(500);digital-
Write(Buzz,LOW);delay(500);digitalWrite(
Buzz,HIGH);delay(500);digitalWrite(
```

```
Buzz,LOW);delay(500);

}
```

```
360bject Alert
330bject Alert
299Bright Light
278Bright Light
280Bright Light
284Bright Light
299Bright Light
296Bright Light
320bject Alert
280bject Alert

✓ Autoscroll
```

At long last, we start estimating the good ways from any deterrent. There will be no alert if the deliberate separation is more than 50cm. Be that as it may, in the event that it is under 50cm the caution will begin by signaling the bell. As the item draws nearer to the ringer the blaring interim will likewise diminish. The closer the article is the quicker the signal will blare. This should be possible by making a postpone that is corresponding to the separation estimated. Since the deferral () in Arduino can't acknowledge factors we need to utilize a for circle which circle dependent on the deliberate separation as demonstrated as follows.

```
if(dist<50)
```

```
{

   Serial.print(dist); Serial.println("Object Alert");

   digitalWrite(Buzz,HIGH);

   for (int i=dist; i>0; i--)

     delay(10);

   digitalWrite(Buzz,LOW);

   for (int i=dist; i>0; i--)

     delay(10);

}
```

Get familiar with estimating the separation utilizing Ultrasonic sensor and Arduino.

The program can be effectively adjusted for your application by changing the worth which we use to look at. You utilize the sequential screen to trouble-shoot if a bogus caution is trigger.

Arduino Blind Stick in Action:

At last it's a great opportunity to test our undertaking. Ensure the associations are done according to the circuit graph and the program is effectively transferred. Presently, control both the circuits utilizing a 9V battery and you should begin to get results. Move the Ultra Sonic sensor closer to question and you will see the Buzzer blaring and this signaling recurrence increments as the stick goes nearer to protest. On the off chance that the LDR is canvassed in dull or if there is an excess of light the ringer will signal. In the event that everything is ordinary the bell won't signal.

When you press the catch on the remote the ringer will give a long signal. I likewise utilize a little stick to mount the total gathering you can utilize a bigger one or a real visually impaired stick and put it in real life.

On the off chance that your ringer is continually blaring it implies the caution is by and large false activated. You can open the sequential screen to check for the parameters and check which is falling in basic and change that. As consistently you can post your concern in the remark area to get help. Expectation you comprehended the venture and delighted in structure something.

Code

```
const int trigger = 3; //Trigger pin of 1st Sesnor
const int echo = 2; //Echo pin of 1st Sesnor
const int Buzz = 13; //Echo pin of 1st Sesnor
const int Remote = A0; //Echo pin of 1st Sesnor
const int Light = A1; //Echo pin of 1st Sesnor
long time_taken;
int dist;
int Signal;
int Intens;
int similar_count;
void setup() {
Serial.begin(9600);
pinMode(Buzz,OUTPUT);
digitalWrite(Buzz,LOW);
pinMode(trigger, OUTPUT);
pinMode(echo, INPUT);
}
/*###Function to calculate distance###*/
```

```
void calculate_distance(int trigger, int echo)
{
digitalWrite(trigger, LOW);
delayMicroseconds(2);
digitalWrite(trigger, HIGH);
delayMicroseconds(10);
digitalWrite(trigger, LOW);
time_taken = pulseIn(echo, HIGH);
dist = time_taken*0.034/2;
if(dist>300)
dist=300;
}
void loop() { //infinite loopy
calculate_distance(trigger,echo);
Signal = analogRead(Remote);
Intens = analogRead(Light);
//Check if Remote is pressed
int temp = analogRead(Remote);
similar_count=0;
while (Signal==temp)
{
Signal = analogRead(Remote);
similar_count++;
}
//If remote pressed
if(similar_count<100)
{
  Serial.print(similar_count); Serial.println("Remote
Pressed");
      digitalWrite(Buzz,HIGH);delay(3000);digital-
```

```
Write(Buzz,LOW);
}
//If very dark
if(Intens<200)
{
 Serial.print(Intens); Serial.println("Bright Light");
   digitalWrite(Buzz,HIGH);delay(200);digitalWrite(
Buzz,LOW);delay(200);digitalWrite(Buzz,HIGH);de-
lay(200);
 digitalWrite(Buzz,LOW);delay(200);
 delay(500);
}

//If very bright
if(Intens>800)
{
 Serial.print(Intens); Serial.println("Low Light");
   digitalWrite(Buzz,HIGH);delay(500);digitalWrite(
Buzz,LOW);delay(500);digitalWrite(Buzz,HIGH);de-
lay(500);
 digitalWrite(Buzz,LOW);delay(500);
}
if(dist<50)
{
 Serial.print(dist); Serial.println("Object Alert");


 digitalWrite(Buzz,HIGH);
 for(int i=dist; i>0; i--)
  delay(10);
 digitalWrite(Buzz,LOW);
```

```
  for (int i=dist; i>0; i--)
    delay(10);


}
//Serial.print("dist=");
//Serial.println(dist);
//Serial.print("Similar_count=");
//Serial.println(similar_count);
//Serial.print("Intens=");
//Serial.println(Intens);
}
```

6.ARDUINO METAL DETECTOR

Metal Detector is a security gadget which is utilized for recognizing metals which can be destructive, at different spots like Airports, shopping centers, films and so forth. Already we have made an extremely basic Metal locator without a microcontroller, presently we are building the Metal Detector utilizing Arduino. In this task, we are going to utilize a curl and capacitor which will be in charge of the recognition of metals. Here we have utilized an Arduino Nano to assemble this metal indicator venture. This is intriguing tasks for all gadgets darlings. Any place this locator distinguishes any metal close to it, the bell starts blaring quickly.

Required Components:

- Connecting jumper wire
- Coil
- Arduino (any)

- 10nF capacitor
- The 1k resistor
- Buzzer
- 330-ohm resistor
- 1N4148 diode
- LED
- Breadboard or PCB
- 9v Battery

Working Concept:

At whatever point some present goes through the loop, it produces an attractive field around it. What's more, the adjustment in the attractive field creates an electric field. Presently as per Faraday's law, in view of this Electric field, a voltage creates over the curl which contradicts the change in attractive field and that is the manner by which Coil builds up the Inductance, implies the produced voltage restricts the expansion in the flow. The unit of Inductance is Henry and recipe to gauge the Inductance is:

$$L = (\mu_o * N^2 * A) / l$$

Where,

L- Inductance in Henries

μ_o- Permeability, its $4\pi*10^{-7}$ for Air

N- Number of turns

A- Inner Core Area (πr^2) in m^2

l- Length of the Coil in meters

At the point when any metal draws close to the curl at that point loop changes its inductance. This adjustment in inductance relies on the metal sort. It's reductions for non-attractive metal and increments for ferromagnetic materials like iron.

Contingent upon the center of the curl, inductance worth changes definitely. In the figure underneath see the air-cored inductors, in these inductors, there will be no strong center. They are essentially loops left noticeable all around. The mechanism of stream of attractive field created by the inductor is nothing or air. These inductors have inductances of less worth.

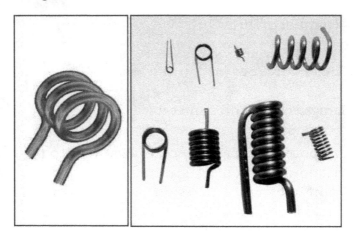

These inductors are utilized when the requirement for estimations of few microHenry. For qualities more noteworthy than couple of milliHenry these are not a reasonable one. In beneath figure you can see an inductor with ferrite center. These Ferrite Core inductor has huge inductance esteem.

Keep in mind the loop twisted here is an air cored one,

so when a metal piece is brought close to the curl, the metal piece goes about as a center for the air cored inductor. By this metal going about as a center, the inductance of the curl changes or increments impressively. With this unexpected increment in inductance of curl the general reactance or impedance of the LC circuit changes by an extensive sum when looked at without the metal piece.

So here in this Arduino Metal Detector Project, we need to discover inductance of the loop to recognize metals. So to do this we have utilized LR circuit (Resistor-Inductor Circuit) that we previously referenced. Here in this circuit, we have utilized a loop having around 20 turns or twisting with a 10cm breadth. We have utilized a vacant tape roll and wind the wire around it to make the curl.

Circuit Diagram:

We have utilized an Arduino Nano for controlling entire this Metal Detector Project. A LED and Buzzer are utilized as metal identification pointer. A Coil and capacitor is utilized for discovery of metals. A sign diode is likewise utilized for diminish the voltage. What's more, a resistor for restricting the current to the Arduino stick.

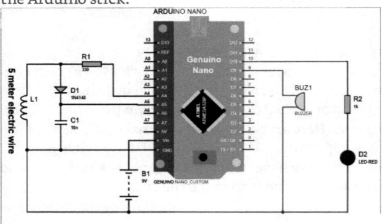

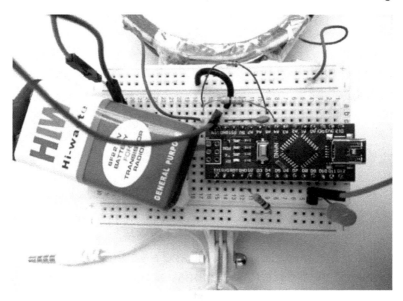

Working Explanation:

Working of this Arduino Metal Detector is bit dubious. Here we give the square wave or heartbeat, created by Arduino, to the LR high pass channel. Because of this, short spikes will be produced by the loop in each progress. The beat length of the produced spikes is corresponding to the inductance of the loop. So with the assistance of these Spike beats we can quantify the inductance of Coil. Yet, here it is hard to quantify inductance unequivocally with that spikes since that spikes are of brief term (approx. 0.5 microseconds) and that is hard to be estimated by Arduino.

So rather than this, we utilized a capacitor which is charged by the rising heartbeat or spike. What's more, it required couple of heartbeats to charge the capacitor to the point where its voltage can be perused by Arduino simple stick A5. At that point Arduino read the voltage of this capacitor by utilizing ADC. In the wake of perusing voltage, capacitor immediately released by making capPin stick as yield and setting it to low. This entire procedure takes around 200 microseconds to finish. For better outcome, we rehash estimation and took a normal of the outcomes. That is the means by which we can quantify the estimated inductance of Coil. In the wake of getting the outcome we move the outcomes to the LED and signal to distinguish the nearness of metal. Check the Complete code given toward the finish of this Article to comprehend the working.

Complete Arduino code is given toward the finish of

this Article. In programming some portion of this task, we have utilized two Arduino pins, one for creating square waves to be sustained in Coil and second simple stick to peruse capacitor voltage. Other than these two pins, we have utilized two more Arduino pins for associating LED and signal.

The total code of Arduino Metal Detector is underneath. You can see that at whatever point it identifies some metal the LED and Buzzer begins to flicker fastly.

Code

```
#define capPin A5
#define buz 9
#define pulsePin A4
#define led 10
long sumExpect=0; //running sum of 64 sums
long ignor=0;  //number of ignored sums
long diff=0;    //difference between sum and avgsum
long pTime=0;
long buzPeriod=0;

void setup()
{
  Serial.begin(9600);
  pinMode(pulsePin, OUTPUT);
  digitalWrite(pulsePin, LOW);
  pinMode(capPin, INPUT);
  pinMode(buz, OUTPUT);
  digitalWrite(buz, LOW);
```

Anbazhagan K

```
 pinMode(led, OUTPUT);
}
void loop()
{
int minval=1023;
int maxval=0;
long unsigned int sum=0;
for (int i=0; i<256; i++)
{
 //reset the capacitor
 pinMode(capPin,OUTPUT);
 digitalWrite(capPin,LOW);
 delayMicroseconds(20);
 pinMode(capPin,INPUT);
 applyPulses();

   //read the charge of capacitor
   int val = analogRead(capPin); //takes 13x8=104
microseconds
 minval = min(val,minval);
 maxval = max(val,maxval);
 sum+=val;

   long unsigned int cTime=millis();
 char buzState=0;
 if(cTime<pTime+10)
 {
  if(diff>0)
   buzState=1;
```

```
   else if(diff<0)
    buzState=2;
  }
  if(cTime>pTime+buzPeriod)
  {
   if(diff>0)
   buzState=1;
   else if(diff<0)
   buzState=2;
   pTime=cTime;
  }
  if(buzPeriod>300)
  buzState=0;
  if(buzState==0)
  {
   digitalWrite(led, LOW);
   noTone(buz);
  }
  else if(buzState==1)
  {
   tone(buz,2000);
   digitalWrite(led, HIGH);
  }

    else if(buzState==2)
  {
   tone(buz,500);
   digitalWrite(led, HIGH);
  }
 }
```

```
//subtract minimum and maximum value to remove
spikes
sum-=minval;
sum-=maxval;

 if(sumExpect==0)
 sumExpect=sum<<6; //set sumExpect to expected
value
 long int avgsum=(sumExpect+32)>>6;
 diff=sum-avgsum;
 if(abs(diff)<avgsum>>10)
 {
  sumExpect=sumExpect+sum-avgsum;
  ignor=0;
 }
 else
  ignor++;
 if(ignor>64)
 {
  sumExpect=sum<<6;
  ignor=0;
 }
 if(diff==0)
  buzPeriod=1000000;
 else
 buzPeriod=avgsum/(2*abs(diff));
}
void applyPulses()
{
  for(int i=0;i<3;i++)
```

```
{
 digitalWrite(pulsePin,HIGH); //take 3.5 uS
 delayMicroseconds(3);
 digitalWrite(pulsePin,LOW); //take 3.5 uS
 delayMicroseconds(3);
 }
}
```

7.ARDUINO RELAY CONTROL TUTORIAL

Driven Blinking is a typical and practically first program for each inserted student or fledgling. In which we squint a LED with having some deferral. So today we are here with a similar task yet here we will utilize an AC bulb rather than typical LED and will squint an AC bulb.

At whatever point we have to associate any AC Appliance in our installed circuits, we utilize a Relay. So in this arduino transfer control instructional exercise we will basically figure out How to interface a Relay with Arduino. Here we are not utilizing any Relay Driver IC like ULN2003 and will just utilize a NPN transistor to control transfer.

Components Required:

- Arduino

- AC appliance or Bulb
- 1k resistor
- BC547 transistor
- Connecting jumper wire
- Breadboard or PCB
- 1n4007 diode
- Power supply
- Screw terminal or terminal block
- 5v or 6v relay

Relay:

Hand-off is an electromagnetic switch, which is constrained by little current, and used to turn ON and OFF moderately a lot bigger current. Means by applying little current we can turn ON the hand-off which enables a lot bigger current to stream. A hand-off is a genuine case of controlling the AC (substitute current) gadgets, utilizing an a lot littler DC current. Generally utilized Relay is SPDT Relay, it has five terminals as underneath:

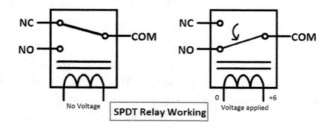

SPDT Relay Working

At the point when there is no voltage applied to

the loop, COM (normal) is associated with NC (typically shut contact). At the point when there is some voltage applied to the curl, the electromagnetic field delivered, which draws in the Armature (switch associated with spring), and COM and NO (regularly open contact) gets associated, which enable a bigger current to stream. Transfers are accessible in numerous appraisals, here we utilized 6V working voltage handoff, which permits 7A-250VAC current to stream.

The transfer is constantly arranged by utilizing a little Driver circuit which comprises a Transistor, Diode and a resistor. Transistor is utilized to enhance the current so full current (from the DC source – 9v battery) can move through a loop to completely energies it. The resistor is utilized to give biasing to the transistor. What's more, Diode is utilized to avoid invert current stream, when the transistor is turned OFF. Each Inductor loop produces equivalent and inverse EMF when turned OFF abruptly, this may make lasting harm parts, so Diode must be utilized to forestall invert current. A Relay module is effectively accessible in the market with all its Driver circuit on the board or you can make it on perf board or PCB like underneath. Here we have utilized 6V Relay module.

Here to turn on the Relay with Arduino we simply need to make that Arduino Pin High (A0 for our situation) where Relay module is associated. Underneath given is Relay Driver Circuit to construct your very own Relay module:

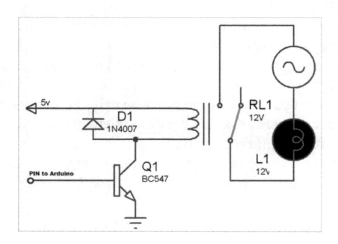

Relay Driver Circuit

Circuit Diagram and Working:

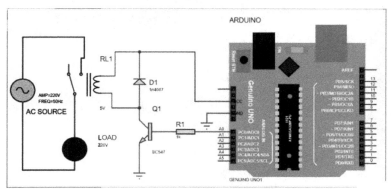

In this Arduino Relay Control Circuit we have utilized Arduino to control the hand-off through a BC547 transistor. We have associated transistor base to Arduino stick A0 through a 1k resistor. An AC bulb is utilized for show. The 12v connector is utilized for driving the circuit.

Working is straightforward, we have to make the RELAY (PIN A0) high to make the Relay module ON as well as make the RELAY stick low to mood killer the Relay Module. The AC light will likewise turn on and off as indicated by Relay.

We just modified the Arduino to make the Relay Pin (A0) High and Low with a deferral of 1 second:

```
void loop()
```

```
{

    digitalWrite(relay, HIGH);

    delay(interval);

    digitalWrite(relay, LOW);

    delay(interval);

}
```

Complete code for Arduino Relay Control is given underneath.

Code

```
// Arduino Relay Control Code
#define relay A0
#define interval 1000
void setup() {
 pinMode(relay, OUTPUT);
}
void loop()
{
  digitalWrite(relay, HIGH);
  delay(interval);
  digitalWrite(relay, LOW);
  delay(interval);
}
```

8.TEMPERATURE CONTROLLED AC HOME APPLIANCES USING ARDUINO AND THERMISTOR

Assume you are sitting in a room and feeling cold and you need your radiator to be consequently turned on, and after that off after some time when room temperature is expanded, at that point this venture help you to control your home apparatuses naturally as per the temperature. Here we are controlling Home AC Appliances with Arduino dependent on the temperature. Here we have utilized Thermistor to peruse the temperature. We as of now interfaced Thermistor with Arduino and showed the Temperature on LCD.

In this instructional exercise, we will append an AC apparatus with Relay and make a temperature controlled home computerization framework utilizing Arduino. It additionally demonstrates the temperature and apparatus status on the 16*2 LCD show associated with the circuit.

Material Required

- Arduino UNO
- 16*2 LCD display
- Relay (5v)
- NTC thermistor 10k
- Light Bulb (CFL)
- Resistors (1k as well as 10k ohms)
- Connecting wires
- Potentiometer (10k)

Circuit Diagram

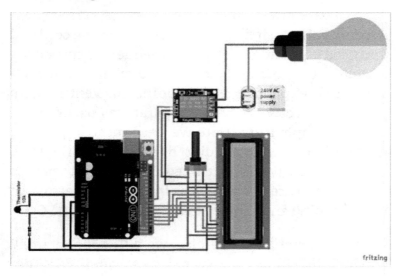

This Temperature based Home Automation System

comprises of different segments like Arduino board, LCD show, Relay, and thermistor. The working mostly relies upon the transfer and thermistor as the temperature expanded the hand-off will be turned on and on the off chance that the temperature diminished beneath the preset worth, at that point Relay will be killed. The Home apparatus associated with the Relay will likewise turns on and off in like manner. Here we have utilized a CFL bulb as AC apparatus. The entire activating procedure and temperature worth setting is performed by the customized Arduino board. It additionally gives us insights regarding the adjustment in temperature in each half second and apparatus status on the LCD screen.

Relay:

Transfer is an electromagnetic switch, which is constrained by little current, and used to turn ON and OFF moderately a lot bigger current. Means by applying little current we can turn ON the transfer which enables a lot bigger current to stream. A transfer is a genuine case of controlling the AC (interchange current) gadgets, utilizing an a lot littler DC current. Generally utilized Relay is SPDT Relay, it has five terminals as underneath:

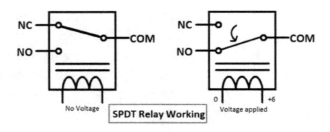

SPDT Relay Working

At the point when there is no voltage applied to the curl, COM (normal) is associated with NC (ordinarily shut contact). At the point when there is some voltage applied to the curl, the electromagnetic field created, which pulls in the Armature (switch associated with spring), and COM and NO (regularly open contact) gets associated, which enable a bigger current to stream. Transfers are accessible in numerous evaluations, here we utilized 5V working voltage hand-off, which permits 7A-250VAC current to stream.

The hand-off is designed by utilizing a little Driver circuit which comprises a Transistor, Diode and a resistor. Transistor is utilized to intensify the current with the goal that full current (from the DC source – 9v battery) can course through a loop to completely energies it. The resistor is utilized to give biasing to the transistor. What's more, Diode is utilized to avoid invert current stream, when the transistor is switched OFF. Each Inductor loop produces equivalent and inverse EMF when turned OFF abruptly, this may make lasting harm segments, so Diode must be utilized to anticipate switch current. A Relay module is effectively accessible in the market with all its Driver circuit on the board or you can make it by utilizing above parts. Here we have utilized 5V Relay module

5v Relay Module

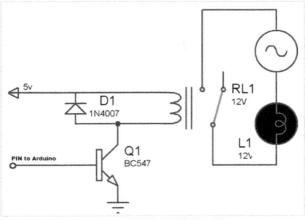

Relay Driver Circuit

Calculating Temperature using Thermistor:

We know from the Voltage divider circuit that:

129

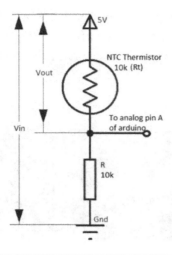

$$V_{out} = (V_{in} * Rt) / (R + Rt)$$

So the estimation of Rt will be:

$$Rt = R(Vin/Vout) - 1$$

Here Rt will be the opposition of the thermistor (Rt) and R will be 10k ohm resistor.

This condition is utilized for the estimation of thermistor obstruction from the deliberate estimation of yield voltage Vo. We can get the estimation of Voltage Vout from the ADC esteem at stick A0 of Arduino as appeared in the Arduino Code given underneath.

Computation of Temperature from the thermistor

obstruction

Numerically the thermistor obstruction must be process with the assistance of the Stein-Hart condition.

$$T = 1 / (A + B^*\ln(Rt) + C^*\ln(Rt)^3)$$

Where, A, B as well as C are the constants, Rt is the thermistor obstruction and ln speaks to log.

The consistent incentive for the thermistor utilized in the undertaking is A = $1.009249522 \times 10\text{-}3$, B = $2.378405444 \times 10\text{-}4$, C = $2.019202697 \times 10\text{-}7$. These steady qualities can be acquired from the adding machine here by entering the three opposition estimations of the thermistor at three distinct temperatures. You can either get these steady qualities legitimately from the datasheet of the Thermistor or you can get three obstruction esteems at various temperature and get the Constants esteems utilizing the given number cruncher.

Along these lines, for computing the temperature we need the estimation of thermistor opposition as it were. Subsequent to getting the estimation of Rt from the figuring given above put the qualities in the Steinhart condition and we will get the estimation of temperature in the unit Kelvin. As there is a minor change in the yield voltage cause change in the temperature.

Anbazhagan K

Arduino code

Complete Arduino Code for this Temperature Controlled Home Appliances is given toward the finish of this article. Here we have clarified few pieces of it.

For performing numerical activity we use Header record "#include <math.h>" and for LCD header document is "#include <LiquidCrystal.h>" and "#define RELAY 8" is utilized to allocate the info stick for a hand-off. We need to relegate the pins of the LCD by utilizing the code.

```
#include <math.h>

#include "LiquidCrystal.h"

#define RELAY 8

LiquidCrystal lcd(6,7,5,4,3,2); // these are in format like LCD(Rs, EN, D4, D5, D6, D7)
```

For arrangement the Relay (as a yield) and LCD at the hour of beginning we need to compose code in the void arrangement part

```
Void setup(){
```

```
lcd.begin(16,2);

lcd.clear();

pinMode(RELAY, OUTPUT);

}
```

For the figuring of temperature by Stein-Hart condition utilizing the electrical opposition of thermistor we play out some straightforward scientific condition in code as clarified in count above:

```
float a = 1.009249522e-03, b = 2.378405444e-04, c = 2.019202697e-07;

float T, logRt, Tf, Tc;

float Thermistor(int Vo) {

logRt = log(10000.0*((1024.0/Vo-1)));

T = (1.0 / (a + b*logRt + c* logRt * logRt * logRt)); // We get the temperature value in Kelvin from this Stein-Hart equation

Tc = T - 273.15;          // Convert Kelvin to Celsius

Tf = (Tc * 1.8) + 32.0;          // Convert Kelvin to
```

```
Fahrenheit

return T;

}
```

In the underneath code the capacity thermistor is perusing the incentive from the simple stick of the Arduino, and print the temperature esteem by playing out the scientific activity

```
lcd.print((Thermistor(analogRead(0))));
```

Also, that worth is taken by the Thermistor capacity and afterward the count is start printing

```
float Thermistor(int Vo)
```

We need to compose the code for the state of turning light ON and OFF as indicated by the temperature as we set the temperature worth like if the temperature increment in excess of 28 degree Celsius the lights will turn ON of if less the lights stay off. So at whatever point the temperature goes above than 28°, we have to make the RELAY (PIN 8) high to make the Relay module ON. What's more, when the temperature goes underneath 28 degrees, we have to make the RELAY stick low to mood killer the Relay Module.

```
if (Tc > 28) digitalWrite(RELAY, HIGH),lcd.setCur-
sor(0,1),lcd.print("Light status:ON "),delay(500);

else if (Tc < 28) digitalWrite(RELAY, LOW),lcd.set-
Cursor(0,1),lcd.print("Light          status:OFF"),de-
lay(500);
```

Working of Temperature Controlled Home Automation System:

To give the stockpile to the Arduino you can control it by means of USB to your workstation or associate 12v connector. A LCD is interfaced with Arduino to show temperature esteems, Thermistor and Relay is associated according to circuit graph. The simple stick (A0) is utilized to check the voltage of thermistor stick at each minute and after the count utilizing Stein-Hart condition through the Arduino code we can get the temperature and show it on LCD in the Celsius and Fahrenheit.

As the temperature expands in excess of 28°C Arduino makes the Relay Module switched On by making the Pin 8 HIGH (where the Relay module is associated) when the temperature goes underneath 28° Arduino turns off the Relay Module by making the Pin LOW. CFL bulb will likewise turn On as well as Off as indicated by Relay module.

This framework can be valuable in Temperature controlled Fan and Automatic AC temperature controller venture.

Likewise check our numerous sorts of Home Automations Projects utilizing various advances and Microcontrollers like:

- DTMF Based Home Automation

- GSM Based Home Automation utilizing Arduino

- PC Controlled Home Automation utilizing Arduino

- Bluetooth Controlled Home Automation utilizing 8051

- IR Remote Controlled Home Automation utilizing Arduino

- home mechanization task utilizing MATLAB and Arduino

- RF Remote Controlled LEDs Using Raspberry Pi

- Advanced cell Controlled Home Automation utilizing Arduino

- Voice Controlled Home Automation utilizing ESP8266 and Android App

- RF based Home Appliances System without Microcontroller

- Raspberry Pi based Smart Phone Controlled Home Automation

Code

```
#include <math.h>
#include "LiquidCrystal.h"
#define RELAY 8
LiquidCrystal lcd(6,7,5,4,3,2);
float A = 1.009249522e-03, B = 2.378405444e-04, C =
2.019202697e-07;
float T,logRt,Tf,Tc;
float Thermistor(int Vo) {
logRt = log(10000.0*((1024.0/Vo-1)));
T = (1.0 / (A + B*logRt + C*logRt*logRt*logRt)); // We
get the temperature value in Kelvin from this Stein-
Hart equation
Tc = T - 273.15;        // Convert Kelvin to Celcius
Tf = (T * 1.8) + 32.0;      // Convert Kelvin to Fahren-
heit
return T;
}
void setup() {
lcd.begin(16,2);
lcd.clear();
pinMode(RELAY, OUTPUT);
}
void loop() {


  lcd.setCursor(0,0);
  lcd.print("Temperature:");
  lcd.print(int(Thermistor(analogRead(0))));
  lcd.print("C ");
  delay(500); // wait 0.5 seconds before sampling tem-
perature again
```

```
if (Tc > 28) digitalWrite(RELAY, HIGH),lcd.setCur-
sor(0,1),lcd.print("Light status:ON "),delay(500);
else if (Tc < 28) digitalWrite(RELAY, LOW),lcd.set-
Cursor(0,1),lcd.print("Light status:OFF"),delay(500);


}
```

9.ARDUINO BASED FIRE FIGHTING ROBOT

As per NCRB, it is evaluated that more than 1.2 lakh passings have been caused on account of flame mishaps in India from 2010-2014. Actually there are a great deal of safeguards taken for Fire mishaps, these common/man-caused calamities to do happen once in a while. In case of a flame breakout, to safeguard individuals and to put out the flame we are compelled to utilize HR which are not sheltered. With the headway of innovation particularly in Robotics it is especially conceivable to supplant people with robots for battling the flame. This would improve the effectiveness of firemen and would likewise keep them from gambling human lives. Today we are going to assemble a Fire Fighting Robot utilizing Arduino, which will consequently detect the flame and start the water siphon

In this venture, we will figure out how to assemble a straightforward robot utilizing Arduino that could move towards the flame and siphon out water around it to put down the flame. It is a straightforward robot that would show us the fundamental idea of apply autonomy; you would have the option to manufacture increasingly advanced robots once you comprehend the accompanying nuts and bolts. So we should begin...

Material Required:

- Arduino UNO

- Servo Motor (SG90)

- Fire sensor or Flame sensor (3 Nos)

- Little Breadboard

- L293D engine Driver module

- A little can

- Robot skeleton with engines just as wheel (any sort)

- Interfacing wires

Working Concept of Fire Fighting Robot:

The primary cerebrum of this venture is the Arduino, however so as to detect fire we utilize the Fire sensor module (fire sensor) that is demonstrated as follows.

As should be obvious these sensors have an IR Receiver (Photodiode) which is used to seperate the flame. How is this conceivable? At the point when fire consumes it radiates a modest quantity of Infrared light, this light will be gotten by the IR recipient on the sensor module. At that point we utilize an Op-Amp to check for change in voltage over the IR Receiver, so that if a flame is distinguished the yield stick (DO) will give 0V(LOW) and if the is no flame the yield stick will be 5V(HIGH).

Thus, we place three such sensors in three ways of the robot to detect on which course the flame is consuming.

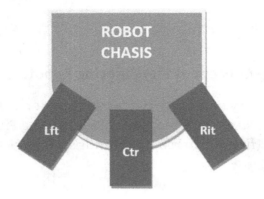

We identify the bearing of the flame we can utilize the engines to move close to the flame by driving our engines through the L293D module. At the point when close to a flame we need to put it out utilizing water. Utilizing a little compartment we can convey water, a 5V siphon is additionally set in the holder and the entire compartment is put over a servo engine with the goal that we can control the bearing wherein the water must be showered. How about we continue with the associations now

Circuit Diagram:

The total circuit outline for this Fire Fighting Robot is given underneath

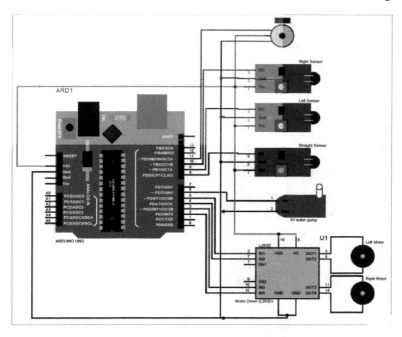

You can either interface all the indicated associations for transferring the program to check the working or you can collect the bot totally and afterward continue with the associations. The two different ways the associations are extremely straightforward and you ought to have the option to hit the nail on the head.

In view of the mechanical undercarriage that you are utilizing you probably won't have the option to utilize a similar sort of holder that I am utilizing. All things considered go through your own inventiveness to set the siphoning framework. Anyway the code will stay same. I utilized a little aluminum can (cool beverages can) to set the siphon inside it and poured water inside it. I at that point gathered the entire can over a servo engine to control the course of water. My robot looks something like this after gathering.

As should be obvious, I have fixed the servo balance to the base of the holder utilizing got stick and have fixed the servo engine with skeleton utilizing stray pieces. We can essentially put the holder over the engine and trigger the siphon inside it to siphon water outside through the cylinder. The entire compartment would then be able to be turned utilizing the servo to control the course of the water.

Programming your Arduino:

When you are prepared with your equipment, you can transfer the Arduino code for some activity. The total program is given toward the finish of this page. Anyway I have additionally clarified couple of significant odds as well as ends here.

As we probably am aware the flame sensor will yield a HIGH when there is fire and will yield a LOW when there is fire. So we need to continue checking these sensor if any flame has happened. In the event that no flame is there we request that the engines remain stop by making every one of the pins high as demonstrated as follows

```
if    (digitalRead(Left_S)    ==1    &&    digit-
alRead(Right_S)==1  &&  digitalRead(Forward_S)
==1) //If Fire not detected all sensors are zero
```

```
{

    //Do not move the robot

    digitalWrite(LM1, HIGH);

    digitalWrite(LM2, HIGH);

    digitalWrite(RM1, HIGH);

    digitalWrite(RM2, HIGH);

}
```

Correspondingly, if there is any flame we can request that the robot move toward that path by pivoting the individual engine. When it arrives at the flame the left and right sensor won't distinguish the flame as it would stand straight in front of the flame. Presently we utilize the variable named "fire" that would execute the capacity to put off the flame.

```
else if (digitalRead(Forward_S) ==0) //If Fire is straight ahead

    {

    //Move the robot forward
```

```
    digitalWrite(LM1, HIGH);

    digitalWrite(LM2, LOW);

    digitalWrite(RM1, HIGH);

    digitalWrite(RM2, LOW);

    fire = true;

}
```

When the variable flame turns out to be valid, the putting out fires robot arduino code will execute the put_off_fire work until the fire is put off. This is finished utilizing the code underneath.

```
while (fire == true)

    {

    put_off_fire();

    }
```

Inside the put_off_fire() we simply need to stop the robot by making every one of the pins high. At the point turn on the siphon to push water outside the holder, while this is done we can likewise utilize the servo engine to pivot the compartment with the goal that the water is part all over consistently. This is finished utilizing the code beneath

```
void put_off_fire()

{

    delay (500);

    digitalWrite(LM1, HIGH);

    digitalWrite(LM2, HIGH);

    digitalWrite(RM1, HIGH);

    digitalWrite(RM2, HIGH);

   digitalWrite(pump, HIGH); delay(500);

    for (pos = 50; pos <= 130; pos += 1) {

    myservo.write(pos);

    delay(10);

  }

 for (pos = 130; pos >= 50; pos -= 1) {
```

```
  myservo.write(pos);

  delay(10);

}

digitalWrite(pump,LOW);

myservo.write(90);

  fire=false;

}
```

Working of Fire Fighting Robot:

It is prescribed to check the yield of the robot in steps instead of running everything together just because. You can manufacture the robot upto the servo engine and check in the event that it can pursue the flame effectively. In that moment you can check if the siphon and the servo engine are working appropriately. Once everything is filling in true to form you can run the program underneath and appreciate the total working of the fireman robot.

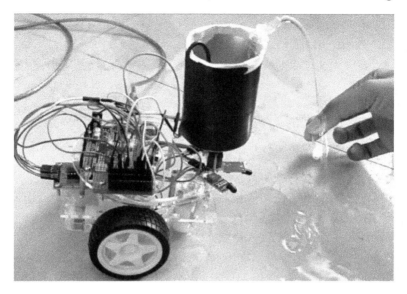

The most extreme separation to which the flame can be distinguished relies upon the size of the flame, for a little matchstick the separation is moderately less. You can likewise utilize the potentiometers over the modules to control the affectability of the robot. I have utilized a power bank to control the robot you can utilize a battery or even power it with a 12V battery.

Expectation you comprehended the undertaking and would appreciate building something comparative.

Look at our Robotics Section to discover progressively cool DIY Robots.

Code

Anbazhagan K

```
/*------ Arduino Fire Fighting Robot Code----- */
#include <Servo.h>
Servo myservo;
int pos = 0;
boolean fire = false;
/*-------defining Inputs------*/
#define Left_S 9    //left sensor
#define Right_S 10    // right sensor
#define Forward_S 8 //forward sensor
/*-------defining Outputs------*/
#define LM1 2    //left motor
#define LM2 3    //left motor
#define RM1 4    // right motor
#define RM2 5    // right motor
#define pump 6
void setup()
{
 pinMode(Left_S, INPUT);
 pinMode(Right_S, INPUT);
 pinMode(Forward_S, INPUT);
 pinMode(LM1, OUTPUT);
 pinMode(LM2, OUTPUT);
 pinMode(RM1, OUTPUT);
 pinMode(RM2, OUTPUT);
 pinMode(pump, OUTPUT);
 myservo.attach(11);
 myservo.write(90);
}
void put_off_fire()
{
  delay (500);
```

```
digitalWrite(LM1, HIGH);
digitalWrite(LM2, HIGH);
digitalWrite(RM1, HIGH);
digitalWrite(RM2, HIGH);
digitalWrite(pump, HIGH); delay(500);
for (pos = 50; pos <= 130; pos += 1) {
myservo.write(pos);
delay(10);
}
for (pos = 130; pos >= 50; pos -= 1) {
myservo.write(pos);
delay(10);
}
digitalWrite(pump,LOW);
myservo.write(90);
fire=false;
}
void loop()
{
 myservo.write(90); //Sweep_Servo();
       if (digitalRead(Left_S) ==1 && digital-
Read(Right_S)==1 && digitalRead(Forward_S) ==1) //
If Fire not detected all sensors are zero
 {
 //Do not move the robot
 digitalWrite(LM1, HIGH);
 digitalWrite(LM2, HIGH);
 digitalWrite(RM1, HIGH);
 digitalWrite(RM2, HIGH);
 }
    else if (digitalRead(Forward_S) ==0) //If Fire is
```

straight ahead

```
{
//Move the robot forward
digitalWrite(LM1, HIGH);
digitalWrite(LM2, LOW);
digitalWrite(RM1, HIGH);
digitalWrite(RM2, LOW);
fire = true;
}
else if (digitalRead(Left_S) ==0) //If Fire is to the left
{
//Move the robot left
digitalWrite(LM1, HIGH);
digitalWrite(LM2, LOW);
digitalWrite(RM1, HIGH);
digitalWrite(RM2, HIGH);
}
  else if (digitalRead(Right_S) ==0) //If Fire is to the
right
{
//Move the robot right
digitalWrite(LM1, HIGH);
digitalWrite(LM2, HIGH);
digitalWrite(RM1, HIGH);
digitalWrite(RM2, LOW);
}
delay(300); //Slow down the speed of robot
  while (fire == true)
  {
  put_off_fire();
  }
```

}

10.INTERFACING THERMISTOR WITH ARDUINO TO MEASURE AND DISPLAY TEMPERATURE ON LCD

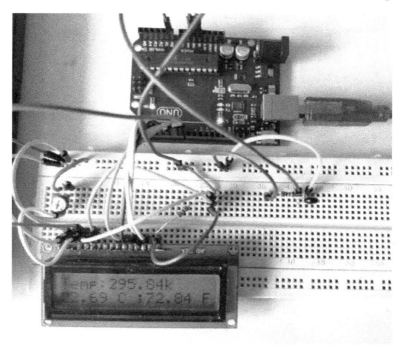

Utilizing a thermistor is simple and modest approach to detect the temperature. Also, to quantify the accurate temperature with thermistor, a microcontroller will be required. So here we are utilizing Arduino with Thermistor to peruse the temperature and a LCD to show the temperature. It is valuable in different ventures like remote climate station, home robotization, and assurance and controlling of mechanical and gadgets equipment's.

We are gonna to interface Thermistor with Arduino and show the temperature on LCD. You can make different electronic circuit based undertakings utilizing thermistor some of them are recorded underneath:

- Temperature Controlled DC Fan utilizing Thermistor

- Alarm utilizing Thermistor

Components Required:

- NTC thermistor 10k
- 10k ohm Resistor
- Arduino (Any version)
- Connecting Wires

Circuit Diagram

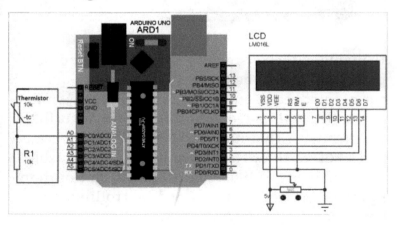

Thermistor gives temperature esteem according to the adjustment in the electrical obstruction in it. In this circuit, the simple stick in the Arduino is associated with the thermistor and can give the ADC esteems just, so the electrical obstruction of thermistor isn't determined straightforwardly. So the circuit is made to resemble a voltage divider circuit as appeared in figure above, by interfacing a known opposition of 10k ohm in arrangement with the NTC. Utilizing this Voltage divider we can get the voltage crosswise over Thermistor and with that voltage we can infer the Resistance of Thermistor right then and there. Lastly we can get the temperature esteem by placing the opposition of thermistor in Stein-Hart condition as clarified in underneath segments.

Thermistor

The key part in this circuit is Thermistor, which has been utilized to distinguish the ascent in temperature. Thermistor is temperature delicate resistor, whose obstruction changes as indicated by the temperature. There are two sorts of thermistor NTC and PTC, we are utilizing a NTC type thermistor. NTC thermistor is a resistor whose obstruction diminishes as ascend in temperature while in PTC it will expand the opposition as ascend in temperature.

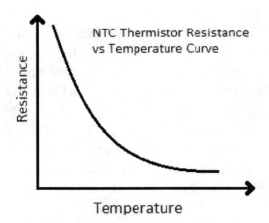

NTC Thermistor Resistance vs Temperature Curve

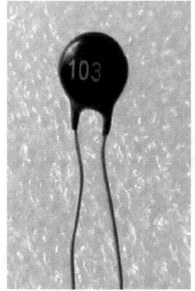

Calculating Temperature using Thermistor:

We know from the Voltage divider circuit that:

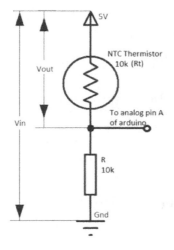

$$V_{out} = (V_{in} * Rt) / (R + Rt)$$

So the estimation of Rt will be:

$$Rt = R (Vin/Vout) - 1$$

Here, Rt will be the obstruction of thermistor and R will be 10k ohm resistor. You can likewise ascertain the qualities from this voltage divider number cruncher.

This condition is utilized for the figuring of thermistor opposition from the deliberate estimation of yield voltage Vo. We can get the estimation of Voltage

Vout from the ADC esteem at stick A0 of Arduino as appeared in the Arduino Code given beneath.

Calculation of Temperature from the thermistor resistance:

Scientifically the thermistor opposition must be register with the assistance of the Stein-Hart condition.

$$T = 1 / (A + B\ln(Rt) + C\ln(Rt)^3)$$

Where, A, B as well as C are the constants, Rt is the thermistor opposition and ln speaks to log.

The steady an incentive for the thermistor utilized in the undertaking is A = 1.009249522×10-3, B = 2.378405444×10-4, C = 2.019202697×10-7. These steady qualities can be acquired from the adding machine here by entering the three opposition estimations of thermistor at three unique temperatures. You can either get these consistent qualities legitimately from the datasheet of the Thermistor or you can get three obstruction esteems at various temperature and get the Constants esteems utilizing the given number cruncher.

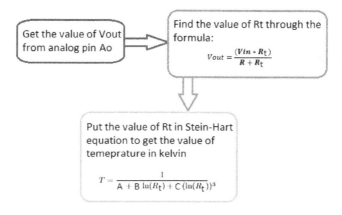

Along these lines, for computing the temperature we need the estimation of thermistor opposition as it were. In the wake of getting the estimation of Rt from the figuring given above put the qualities in the Steinhart condition and we will get the estimation of temperature in the unit kelvin. As there is minor change in the yield voltage cause change in the temperature.

Arduino thermistor code

Complete Arduino Code for Interfacing Thermistor with Arduino is given toward the finish of this article. Here we have clarified few pieces of it.

For performing scientific activity we use Header record "#include <math.h>" and for LCD header document is "#include <LiquidCrystal.h>". We need to appoint the pins of the LCD by utilizing the code

```
LiquidCrystal lcd(44,46,40,52,50,48);
```

For arrangement the LCD at the hour of beginning we need to compose code in the void arrangement part

```
Void setup(){

 lcd.begin(16,2);

 lcd.clear();

}
```

For the count of temperature by Stein-Hart condition utilizing the electrical opposition of thermistor we play out some straightforward scientific condition in code as clarified in figuring above:

```
float a = 1.009249522e-03, b = 2.378405444e-04, c = 2.019202697e-07;

float T,logRt,Tf,Tc;

float Thermistor(int Vo) {

 logRt = log(10000.0*((1024.0/Vo-1)));
```

```
T = (1.0 / (A + B*logRt + C*logRt*logRt*logRt));//
We get the temperature value in Kelvin from this
Stein-Hart equation

Tc = T - 273.15;          // Convert Kelvin to Celsius


Tf = (Tc * 1.8) + 32.0;          // Convert Kelvin to
Fahrenheit

return T;

}
```

In the beneath code the capacity thermistor is per-using the incentive from the simple stick of the Arduino,

```
lcd.print((Thermistor(analogRead(0))));
```

furthermore, that worth is taken in the code beneath and afterward the count is start printing

```
float Thermistor(int Vo)
```

Measuring Temperature with Thermistor and Arduino:

To give the stockpile to the Arduino you can control it through USB to your workstation or interfacing 12v connector. A LCD is interfaced with Arduino to show temperature esteems and Thermistor is associated according to circuit graph. The simple stick (A0) is utilized to check the voltage of thermistor stick at each minute and after the computation utilizing Stein-Hart condition through the Arduino code we can get the temperature and show it on LCD in the Celsius and Fahrenheit.

Code

```
#include <math.h>
#include "LiquidCrystal.h"
```

```
LiquidCrystal lcd(44,46,40,52,50,48);
float A = 1.009249522e-03, B = 2.378405444e-04, C =
2.019202697e-07;
float T,logRt,Tf,Tc;
float Thermistor(int Vo) {
logRt = log(10000.0*((1024.0/Vo-1)));
 T = (1.0 / (A + B*logRt + C*logRt*logRt*logRt)); // We
get the temperature value in Kelvin from this Stein-
Hart equation
Tc = T - 273.15;        // Convert Kelvin to Celcius
Tf = (Tc * 1.8) + 32.0;       // Convert Kelvin to Fahren-
heit
 return T;
}
void setup(){
lcd.begin(16,2);
lcd.clear();
}
void loop()
{
lcd.setCursor(0,0);
lcd.print("Temp:");
lcd.print((Thermistor(analogRead(0))));
lcd.print("k ");


lcd.setCursor(0,1);
lcd.print((Tc));
lcd.print(" C ;");
lcd.setCursor(9,1);
```

Anbazhagan K

```
lcd.print((Tf));
lcd.print(" F");
delay(800);
}
```

www.ingramcontent.com/pod-product-compliance
Lightning Source LLC
Chambersburg PA
CBHW071128050326
40690CB00008B/1380